Written with beginners and researchers in mind, this easy-to-follow guide focuses on **Google Workspace**, breaking down its features into simple, step-by-step lessons. You'll learn practical skills that will help you work smarter, not harder.

Whether you're a student, a professional, or someone just getting started with Google's tools, this book will equip you with the knowledge and confidence to navigate Google Workspace with ease. Let this guide be your key to unlocking productivity, creativity, and efficiency in both your personal and professional life.

Table of Contents

PART 1: Getting Started with Google Workspace

Chapter 1: Introduction to Google Workspace

Google Workspace is a comprehensive suite of productivity and collaboration tools designed to help individuals, teams, and organizations streamline their workflow. It includes cloud-based applications such as Gmail, Google Drive, Google Docs, Google Sheets, Google Meet, and more, all seamlessly integrated to enhance communication and collaboration. With Google Workspace, you can create, store, share, and collaborate on documents, spreadsheets, presentations, and other files from anywhere with an internet connection.

Google Workspace makes it easy to collaborate in real-time, share files securely, and manage your business or personal tasks effectively. It's a one-stop solution for managing communication, file storage, calendar management, and even online meetings.

Key Apps in Google Workspace:

- **Gmail**: Professional email service with advanced features.
- **Google Drive**: Cloud storage for all your files, with easy sharing and collaboration.
- **Google Docs/Sheets/Slides**: Word processing, spreadsheets, and presentations, all in the cloud.
- **Google Meet**: Video conferencing for remote collaboration.
- **Google Calendar**: Schedule and manage appointments and events.
- **Google Keep**: Note-taking and to-do lists.
- **Google Forms**: Easy creation of surveys and quizzes.

Google Workspace vs. Free Google Apps

While Google Workspace and the free Google apps (such as Gmail, Google Drive, and Google Docs) share some similarities, there are several key differences between the two:

1. **Business Features**:
   - **Google Workspace** offers premium features like custom domain emails (yourname@yourcompany.com), advanced admin controls, and more collaborative tools, ideal for businesses and teams.

- Free Google Apps have limitations in these areas, including a lack of custom domains and fewer management controls for organizational setups.

2. **Storage and Collaboration**:
   - **Google Workspace** offers enhanced cloud storage (starting at 30 GB per user) and the ability to collaborate on documents in real-time with your team, making it easier to track changes and manage multiple contributors.
   - **Free Google Apps** only provide limited storage (15 GB) and are designed more for personal use rather than team collaboration.

3. **Security and Admin Controls**:
   - **Google Workspace** includes advanced security features like 2-step verification, security key management, and more, along with the ability to manage user permissions and access within a team or organization.
   - **Free Google Apps** do not provide these advanced security measures or administrative tools.

4. **Support**:
   - **Google Workspace** provides 24/7 customer support, with dedicated help from Google support agents, as well as a host of admin and troubleshooting resources.
   - **Free Google Apps** rely on community support and limited help resources.

Benefits of Google Workspace for Individuals & Businesses

Google Workspace offers a wealth of advantages for both individuals and businesses. Here's a breakdown of how it can benefit each group:

For Individuals:

- **Access from Anywhere**: Whether you're at home, in a coffee shop, or traveling, you can access all your files, emails, and documents from any device with an internet connection.

- **Seamless Collaboration**: If you're working on group projects or planning events, you can collaborate in real-time using tools like Google Docs, Google Sheets, and Google Meet. This allows for instant feedback and updates without the need for constant back-and-forth emails.
- **Organization**: With tools like Google Calendar and Google Keep, individuals can easily stay on top of their personal tasks and appointments. You can set reminders, create to-do lists, and manage your time more effectively.

For Businesses:

- **Professional Email**: With Google Workspace, businesses can create email accounts using their company's custom domain, adding a professional touch to communications.
- **Team Collaboration**: Google Workspace enhances collaboration with tools such as **shared drives**, **Google Meet**, and real-time editing in **Google Docs/Sheets/Slides**, fostering teamwork and productivity.
- **Security**: Businesses can benefit from high-level security measures like data encryption, single sign-on (SSO), and advanced admin controls to manage team access and permissions.
- **Cloud Storage**: With more storage space and the ability to share files easily, team members can collaborate on documents, store important files, and access them whenever needed.

Subscription Plans & Pricing Explained

Google Workspace offers several pricing plans tailored to different needs, ranging from individual use to large enterprises. Each plan comes with unique features and pricing, designed to fit various usage scenarios.

Google Workspace Plans:

1. **Business Starter**:
    - Price: $6 per user/month

- Features: 30 GB cloud storage per user, professional email, Google Meet (1-on-1 meetings, 100 participants), security features like 2-step verification, and Google Drive for easy file sharing and storage.

2. **Business Standard**:
   - Price: $12 per user/month
   - Features: 2 TB cloud storage per user, more advanced Google Meet capabilities (up to 150 participants), enhanced admin controls, and better collaboration features with shared drives.

3. **Business Plus**:
   - Price: $18 per user/month
   - Features: 5 TB cloud storage per user, advanced security features, eDiscovery, and audit reports for compliance.

4. **Enterprise**:
   - Price: Custom pricing
   - Features: Unlimited storage, enhanced security, 24/7 support, advanced reporting, and more.

Signing Up for Google Workspace (Step-by-Step)

Getting started with Google Workspace is simple. Follow these steps to sign up:

Step 1: Visit the Google Workspace Website
Go to https://workspace.google.com.

Step 2: Click "Get Started"
On the homepage, click the **Get Started** button to begin the sign-up process.

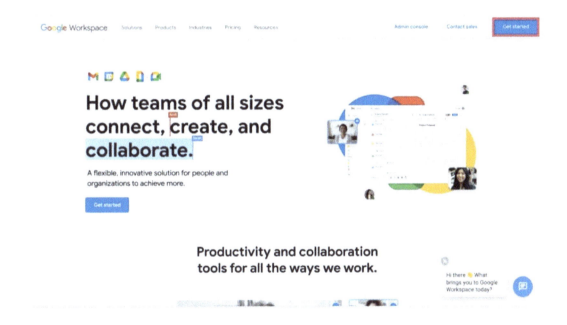

Step 3: Enter Your Business Name and Contact Information
Fill out the form with your business name, number of employees, and your contact information. Google will ask for a valid email address to send you account information.

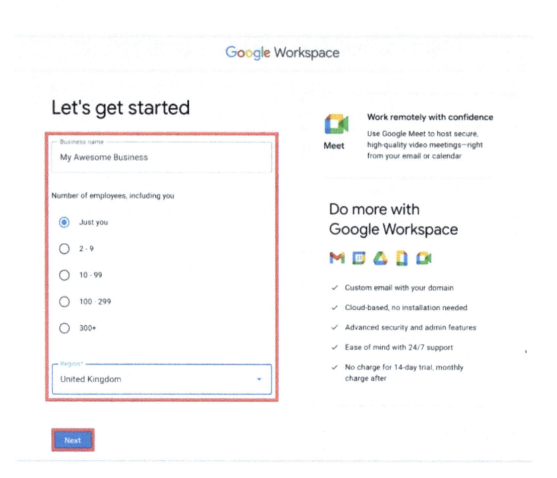

Step 4: Choose Your Plan
Select the plan that best suits your needs. Google will prompt you with options to pick between Business Starter, Standard, Plus, or Enterprise. Choose based on the number of employees and storage needs.

Step 5: Set Up Your Domain
If you already have a domain, enter it here. If not, you can purchase a domain directly through Google during the sign-up process.

Step 6: Create Your User Accounts
Enter the names and email addresses of your team members who will use Google Workspace. You can create individual accounts for each user and assign appropriate roles.

Step 7: Set Up Your Payment

Provide your payment information, including credit card details, and complete the checkout process. Google will charge you based on the plan you selected.

Exploring the Google Workspace Dashboard

Once you've signed up and logged in, you'll be directed to the **Google Workspace Admin Console**. This is your control center where you can manage user accounts, apps, settings, and more.

- **Admin Console Overview**: The dashboard is divided into sections like **Users**, **Apps**, **Security**, **Billing**, and **Reports**.
- **Adding Users**: In the **Users** section, you can add new users, assign roles, and set up access to specific apps.
- **Managing Apps**: Under **Apps**, you can enable or disable apps like Gmail, Google Meet, and Google Drive, customizing what's available to your team.

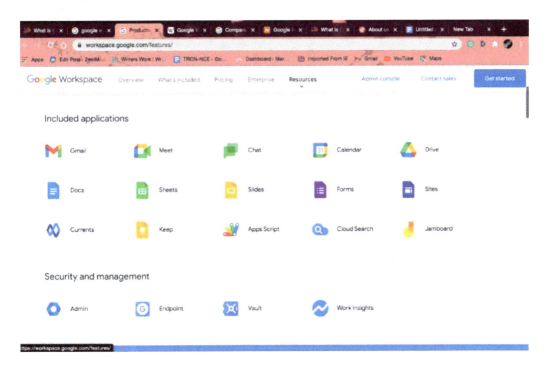

How to Access & Switch Between Google Tools

Accessing Google tools is simple and efficient with Google Workspace:

1. **Access Google Tools**:
   All your apps, including Gmail, Drive, Docs, Sheets, etc., are available in the **Google Apps menu**, located at the top-right of your screen (the 9-dot grid). Click this icon, and you'll see a list of apps you can access.

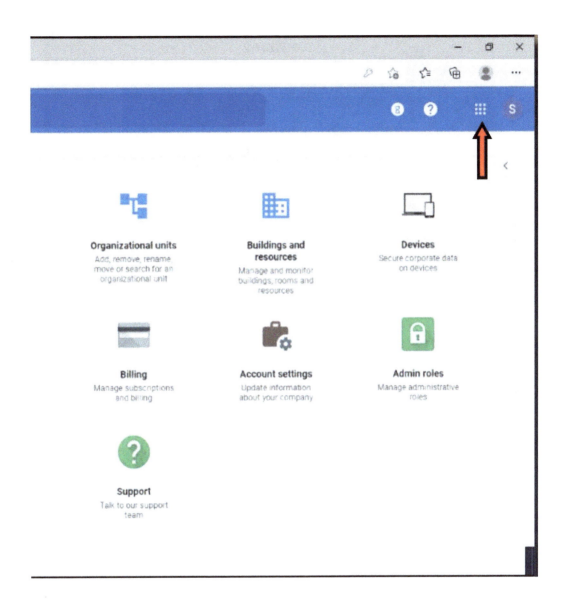

2. **Switch Between Tools**:
   Once you're inside an app (e.g., Gmail), simply click on the **Google Apps menu** again to switch to another tool, like **Google Calendar** or **Google Docs**. Each tool opens in a new tab, allowing you to multitask with ease.

Summary

In this section, you've learned about:

- What Google Workspace is and how it differs from free Google apps.
- The benefits of using Google Workspace for both individuals and businesses.
- The different subscription plans and pricing options available.
- How to sign up for Google Workspace and get started with your account.
- Navigating the **Google Workspace Dashboard** and switching between tools easily.

Chapter 2: Setting Up & Managing Your Google Account

A **Google Account** is your key to accessing all of Google's services, from Gmail and Google Drive to YouTube and Google Calendar. It's important to set it up correctly from the beginning to ensure a smooth experience when using Google Workspace.

Step 1: Visit the Google Account Creation Page

Go to https://accounts.google.com/signup.

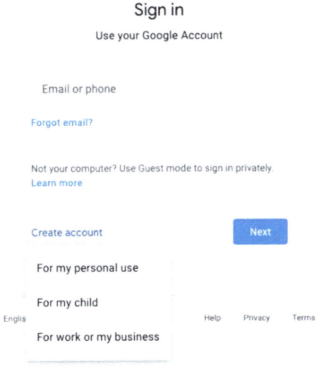

Step 2: Enter Your Personal Information

Fill in the required fields, including:

- **First Name and Last Name**: These will appear on your email and profile.
- **Username**: This will be your unique email address (e.g., yourname@gmail.com). If your desired username is already taken, Google will suggest alternatives or you can create your own.
- **Password**: Create a strong password that is easy for you to remember but difficult for others to guess. Google will recommend a combination of letters, numbers, and symbols for enhanced security.

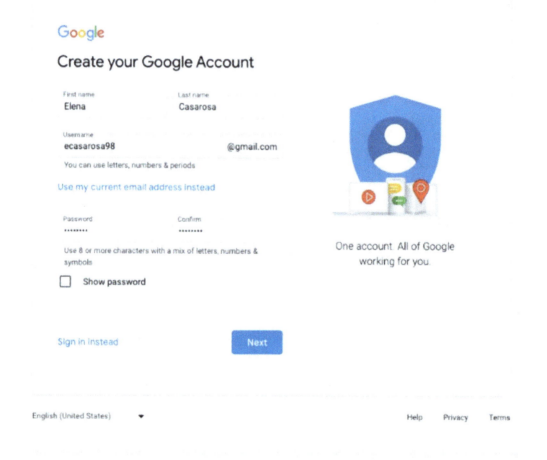

Step 3: Confirm Your Information
After filling out the details, click **Next** to confirm your username and password. Google may ask you to verify your email address by sending a code to the address you provided.

Step 4: Set Up Recovery Options
Google will ask for a recovery email and phone number. These are optional but highly recommended. They allow you to recover your account in case you forget your password or need to verify your identity.

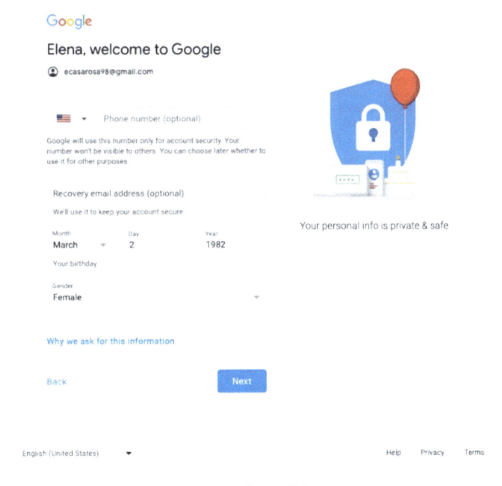

Step 5: Agree to Google's Terms and Conditions
Read through the **Privacy & Terms** document. You need to accept Google's

terms in order to create your account. Once you've reviewed the terms, click **I Agree**.

Google

Privacy and Terms

To create a Google Account, you'll need to agree to the Terms of Service below.

In addition, when you create an account, we process your information as described in our Privacy Policy, including these key points:

Data we process when you use Google

- When you set up a Google Account, we store information you give us like your name, email address, and telephone number.
- When you use Google services to do things like write a message in Gmail or comment on a YouTube video, we store the information you create.
- When you search for a restaurant on Google Maps or watch a video on YouTube, for example, we process information about that activity – including information like the video you watched, device IDs, IP addresses, cookie data, and location.
- We also process the kinds of information described above when you use apps or sites that use Google services like ads, Analytics, and the YouTube video player.

You're in control of the data we collect & how it's used

Step 6: Complete Your Account Setup

After agreeing to the terms, your account will be set up, and you can access all of Google's services.

Setting Up Your Profile Picture & Personal Information

A personalized account not only makes it easier for others to recognize you but also adds a touch of professionalism. Here's how to set up your profile picture and personal information.

Step 1: Go to Your Google Account

Once you're logged in, click on your **profile icon** (or the default avatar) in the top-right corner. Then, click on **Manage Your Google Account**.

Step 2: Update Your Profile Picture

Under the **Personal Info** tab, you'll see the option to add or change your profile picture. Click on the **Camera icon** next to the default avatar, and you can upload a new photo from your computer or choose one from your Google Photos.

Step 3: Update Your Personal Information

In the **Personal Info** section, you can update:

- **Name**: Make sure this is accurate as it will appear in emails and other Google services.
- **Birthday**: This helps Google provide age-appropriate features and content.
- **Gender**: You can choose to leave this blank or set it to your preference.
- **Contact Information**: Here, you can add or update your phone number, recovery email, and physical address if necessary.

Step 4: Review & Save Changes

Once you've updated your details, review them to ensure they're correct. Click **Save** to confirm the changes.

Managing Google Account Settings (Security, Privacy, & Notifications)

Your **Google Account Settings** give you full control over your account's security, privacy, and notifications. Let's break down how to manage each of these elements.

Step 1: Access Your Account Settings

In your Google Account, go to the **Security**, **Privacy**, and **Notifications** tabs to customize your settings.

Step 2: Manage Security Settings

- **Two-Step Verification**: To add an extra layer of security, enable **two-step verification**. This requires you to enter a code sent to your phone whenever you sign in, making it harder for unauthorized users to access your account.
  - ○ **How to Set Up**: In the **Security** tab, find **2-Step Verification** and follow the on-screen instructions to set it up.
- **Recovery Information**: Make sure your recovery email and phone number are up to date in case you need to recover your account.
- **Recent Security Events**: Review any recent security events in the **Security Checkup** section. Google will notify you if there were any suspicious activities or login attempts on your account.

Step 3: Manage Privacy Settings

- **Data & Personalization**: This section allows you to manage the data Google collects about you and how it is used across different services. You can control whether Google collects data for ads, search history, YouTube videos, and more.

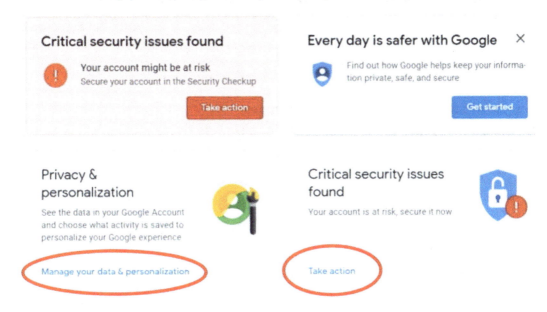

- o **How to Customize**: In the **Privacy** tab, click on **Manage Your Privacy Settings** to customize your preferences.
- **Ad Personalization**: You can turn off personalized ads if you prefer not to have Google track your interests for advertising purposes.

Step 4: Manage Notification Settings

- **Email and App Notifications**: Under **Notifications**, you can choose how Google sends you updates about your account, product updates, or promotional emails.
  - o **How to Customize**: Go to the **Notifications** section of your account settings and select which types of notifications you want to receive.

Understanding Google Storage Plans & Upgrading Storage

Google offers cloud storage through **Google Drive**, which is part of your Google Account. By default, you get **15 GB of free storage** for all your data, including Gmail attachments, photos, and files in Google Drive. However, as your needs grow, you may want to upgrade your storage plan.

Step 1: Check Your Current Storage Usage
To see how much storage you have left, go to **Google Drive** and look at the bottom of the page to see the storage bar. You can also visit **Google One** to get a more detailed breakdown of your storage usage across Google services (Drive, Gmail, and Google Photos).

Step 2: Google Storage Plans
If you find that 15 GB isn't enough, you can upgrade to a paid plan through **Google One**. Here are the available options:

- **100 GB Plan**: $1.99/month
- **200 GB Plan**: $2.99/month
- **2 TB Plan**: $9.99/month

Step 3: Upgrade Your Storage
To upgrade, go to https://one.google.com or directly through Google Drive. Click on the **Upgrade Storage** button to choose a plan that fits your needs. You can then pay via credit card, and the new storage capacity will be available immediately.

Step 4: Additional Storage Features
Google One also offers additional perks for subscribers, such as:

- Family sharing (up to 5 people can share the same storage plan).
- Access to Google experts for help.
- Discounts on select Google products and services.

Summary

In this section, you've learned:

- How to create a **Google Account** and set it up for first-time use.
- How to personalize your profile picture and personal details.
- How to manage the **security**, **privacy**, and **notification** settings for your account.
- How to **understand and upgrade your Google storage** to accommodate your growing file and email needs.

Chapter 3: Google Workspace Security & Privacy Settings

Google Workspace provides robust security and privacy features to protect your account and data. In this section, you will learn how to **enhance your account security, manage recovery options, adjust privacy settings, and review connected apps** to ensure your account remains secure.

Enabling Two-Factor Authentication (2FA)

Two-Factor Authentication (2FA), also known as **2-Step Verification**, adds an extra layer of protection by requiring a second verification step in addition to your password. This prevents unauthorized access even if someone manages to steal your password.

Why Enable 2FA?

- **Prevents unauthorized logins** by requiring a second verification step.
- **Adds security to sensitive Google Workspace data**, especially for businesses.
- **Protects against phishing attacks** that try to steal passwords.

How to Enable 2FA on Your Google Account

Step 1: Open Google Account Security Settings

1. Sign in to your **Google Account** at
   https://myaccount.google.com/security.

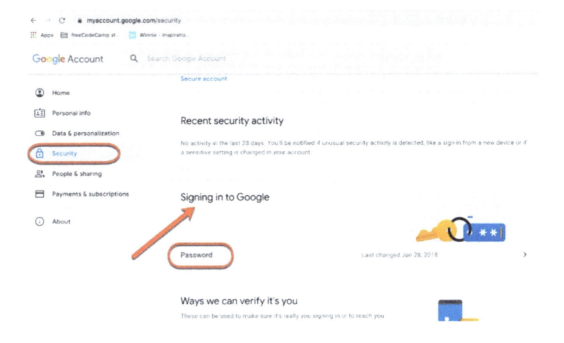

2. Click on **"2-Step Verification"**.

Security Checkup

1 issue found

2-Step Verification
Add a backup second step ⌄

Your devices
2 signed-in devices ⌄

Recent security events
5 recent events ⌄

Step 2: Start the Setup Process

1. Click **"Get Started"**.
2. Enter your **Google account password** for verification.

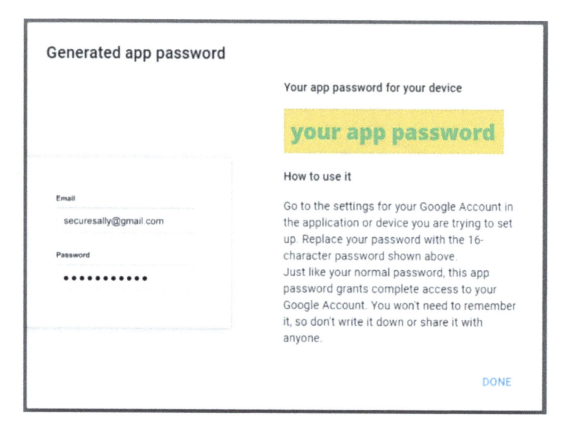

Step 3: Choose Your 2FA Verification Method

Google provides multiple options for verification:

- **SMS or Voice Call**: Google will send a one-time code to your mobile phone.
- **Google Authenticator App**: A more secure method that generates time-sensitive codes.
- **Backup Codes**: Printable codes for emergency access.
- **Security Key**: A physical USB or Bluetooth device that acts as a key.

Step 4: Verify Your 2FA Method

1. If using SMS or a phone call, enter the verification code you receive.

2. If using an app, scan the QR code with the **Google Authenticator** app.
3. Click **Turn On** to activate 2FA.

Step 5: Set Up Backup Options

- Add **backup phone numbers** in case your primary phone is unavailable.
- Download **backup codes** and store them safely for emergency access.

From now on, every time you sign in, Google will require your password **and** the second authentication step for added security.

Managing Google Account Recovery Options

Having the right recovery options ensures that you can regain access to your account if you forget your password or suspect unauthorized access.

Why Are Recovery Options Important?

- **Prevents permanent lockout** if you forget your password.
- **Allows quick recovery** in case of suspicious activity.
- **Ensures business continuity** for professional Google Workspace accounts.

How to Set Up or Update Recovery Information

Step 1: Go to Google Account Recovery Settings

1. Visit **https://myaccount.google.com/security**.
2. Scroll down to the **"Ways We Can Verify It's You"** section.

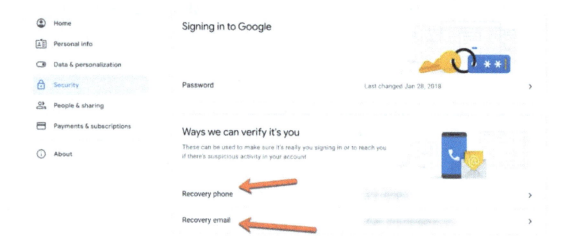

Step 2: Add or Update Recovery Information

- **Recovery Email**: This is an alternative email where Google will send recovery links.
  - Click **"Recovery Email"**, enter a valid email address, and verify it.
- **Recovery Phone Number**: Google will send a verification code via text or call.
  - Click **"Recovery Phone"**, enter your phone number, and confirm.

Step 3: Test Your Recovery Options

- Go to Google Account Recovery and try recovering your account using the options you set up.
- If the process works smoothly, your recovery settings are properly configured.

Adjusting Privacy & Data Sharing Settings

Google collects data to improve its services, but you can control how much information you share. Adjusting these settings ensures your **personal or business data** remains secure.

How to Adjust Privacy Settings

Step 1: Open Google Privacy Settings

1. Sign in to https://myaccount.google.com/privacycheckup.
2. Click **"Privacy Checkup"** to review and adjust your settings.

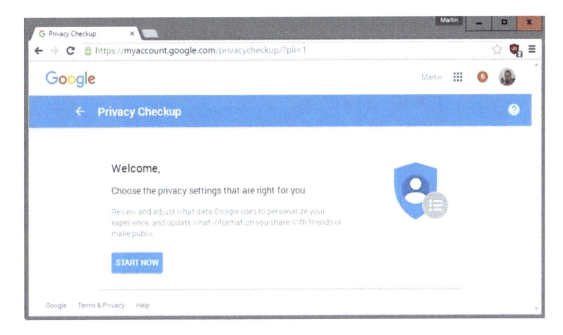

Step 2: Manage Activity Controls

Google tracks your activities for a personalized experience. You can **disable tracking** for:

- **Web & App Activity**: Stops Google from saving your browsing history.
- **Location History**: Prevents Google from tracking your device location.
- **YouTube History**: Stops tracking videos you watch.

To disable any of these:

1. Click on the setting (e.g., **Web & App Activity**).
2. Toggle **OFF** the option to stop tracking.

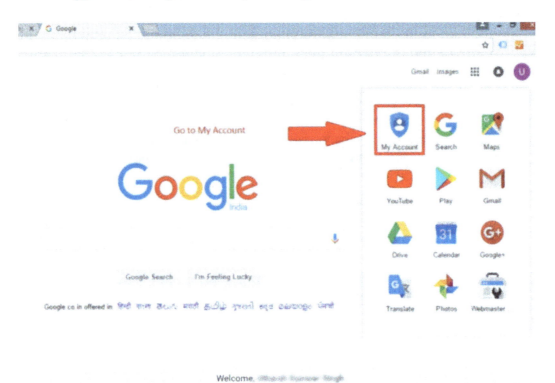

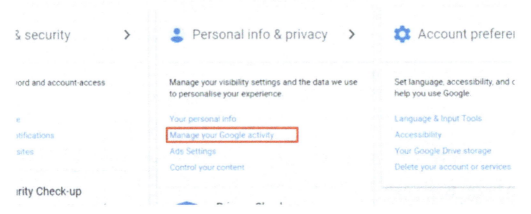

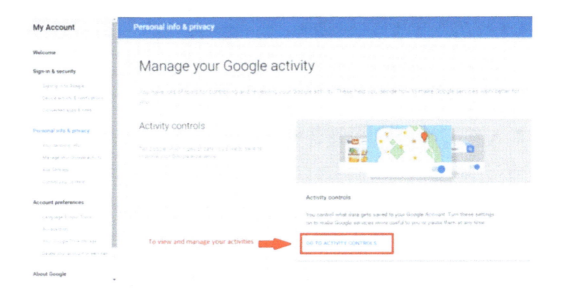

Step 3: Manage Data Sharing Preferences

- Under **"Data & Personalization"**, go to **"Ad Personalization"**.

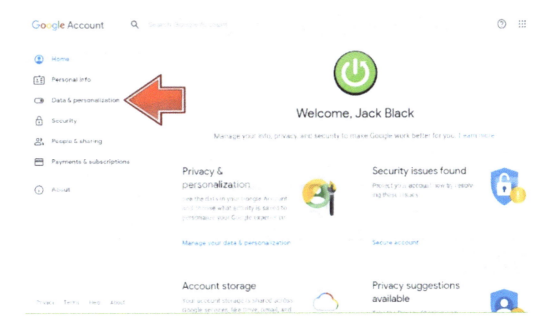

- Toggle **OFF** to stop Google from using your data for personalized ads.
- Under **"Third-party apps with account access"**, remove any apps that don't need access.

Step 4: Set Up Auto-Delete for Data

- Click **"Manage Your Data & Privacy"**.
- Select **"Auto-delete"** for Web Activity, Location History, and YouTube History.
- Choose **3 months, 18 months, or 36 months** for automatic deletion.

Reviewing & Managing Connected Apps

Over time, you might have given third-party apps permission to access your Google account. It's important to review and remove apps that no longer need access.

Why Review Connected Apps?

- **Prevents security risks** from outdated or untrusted apps.
- **Limits data exposure** to external services.
- **Improves account control** by revoking unnecessary permissions.

How to Check & Remove Connected Apps

Step 1: Open the Connected Apps Page

1. Go to **https://myaccount.google.com/security**.
2. Scroll down to **"Third-party apps with account access"**.

Step 2: Review App Permissions

- Look at the list of connected apps.
- Click on each app to see **what data it can access**.

Step 3: Remove Apps You No Longer Use

- Click on an app, then select **"Remove Access"**.
- Confirm the removal if prompted.

Step 4: Enable App Security Restrictions (For Business Accounts)

If you use Google Workspace for business:

1. Visit **Admin Console → Security**.
2. Set up **OAuth app restrictions** to limit which apps can connect.

PART 2: Communication & Collaboration Tools

Chapter 4: Mastering Gmail – The Ultimate Email Tool

G mail is the heart of Google Workspace, providing a **powerful, intuitive, and feature-rich** email platform. Whether you're an individual user or a business professional, mastering Gmail can help you **communicate efficiently, stay organized, and enhance productivity**.

This chapter will walk you through **Gmail's interface, composing emails, organizing your inbox, using shortcuts, scheduling messages, and managing spam**—all in a **clear, step-by-step format**.

Gmail Interface Overview

Before diving into Gmail's features, it's essential to understand the **interface layout**.

Navigating the Gmail Dashboard

1. **Sign in to Gmail**
   - Go to mail.google.com and log in with your Google Workspace credentials.
2. **Explore the Main Sections**
   - **Inbox**: Displays received emails, sorted by primary, social, or promotions (by default).
   - **Compose Button**: Found on the left sidebar, used to create a new email.
   - **Labels & Folders**: Found on the left sidebar, used for organizing emails.

- o **Search Bar**: Located at the top, allowing quick searches using filters.
- o **Settings (⚙ Icon)**: Found in the top-right corner, providing access to customization options.

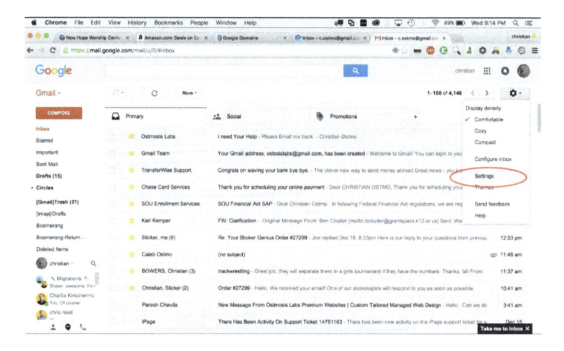

Understanding Email Categories

Gmail automatically **categorizes** emails into:

- **Primary** – Important emails from contacts and businesses.
- **Social** – Notifications from social media platforms.
- **Promotions** – Marketing emails and promotional offers.

Composing & Formatting Emails Effectively

Sending a well-structured email improves **clarity, professionalism, and engagement**.

How to Compose an Email

1. **Click the "Compose" button** (bottom-left of the screen).

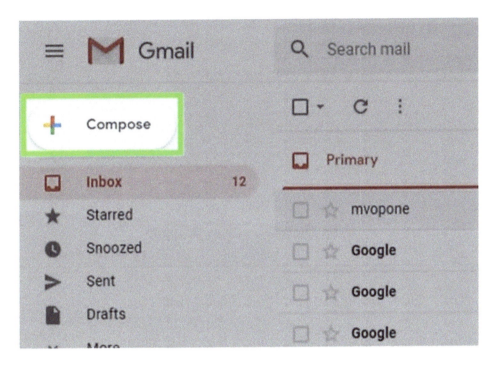

2. **Enter the recipient's email address** in the **"To" field**.
3. **Use "Cc" (Carbon Copy) or "Bcc" (Blind Carbon Copy)** when sending to multiple recipients.
4. **Add a clear subject line** that summarizes the email content.
5. **Write your message** in the body section.

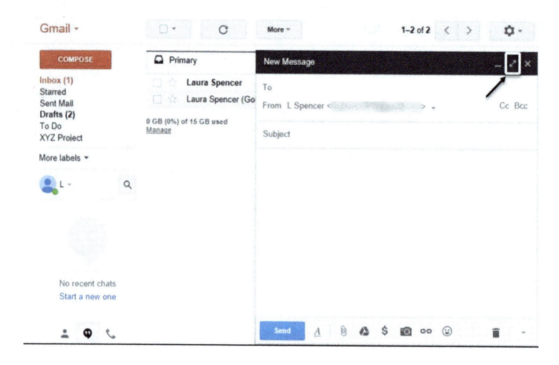

Formatting Your Email for Clarity & Readability

Use the formatting toolbar at the bottom of the email composer:

- **Bold, Italic, Underline** – Highlight important text.
- **Bullets & Numbered Lists** – Organize information clearly.
- **Hyperlinks** – Add clickable links.
- **Text Alignment & Indentation** – Improve readability.

Attaching Files & Images

- Click the **paperclip** 📎 icon to attach files.
- Drag and drop files directly into the email.
- Use **Google Drive integration** for larger attachments.

Sending the Email

- Click **"Send"** once your email is ready.
- Click **"Undo"** (appears briefly) to recall a sent email if needed.

Organizing Emails with Labels, Filters & Stars

Gmail provides powerful tools to **organize, prioritize, and automate email management**.

Using Labels to Categorize Emails

Labels work like folders but allow **multiple categorizations** for the same email.

How to Create a New Label:

1. Click on the **"More"** option in the left sidebar.
2. Select **"Create new label"** and enter a name.
3. Click **"Create"** to add it to your Gmail.

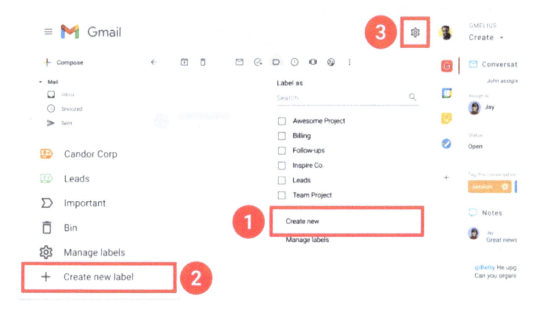

How to Apply Labels to Emails:

- Open an email, click **"Labels"** (tag icon), and choose a label.

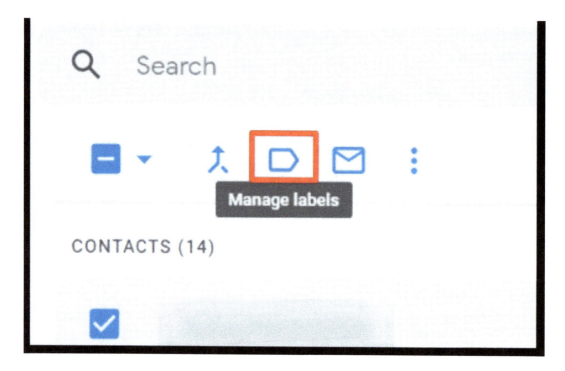

Using Filters to Automate Email Sorting

Filters automatically **sort incoming emails** into specific labels, mark them as read, or forward them.

How to Create an Email Filter:

1. Click the **search bar** at the top of Gmail.
2. Enter criteria (e.g., sender, keywords, attachments).
3. Click **"Create filter"** and choose an action (e.g., apply a label, mark as important).
4. Click **"Create Filter"** to finalize.

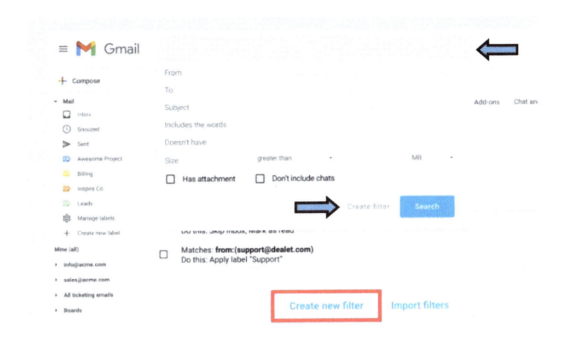

Using Stars & Importance Markers

- Click the ★ **Star icon** next to an email to highlight important messages.
- Use **priority markers (▸)** to identify important emails.

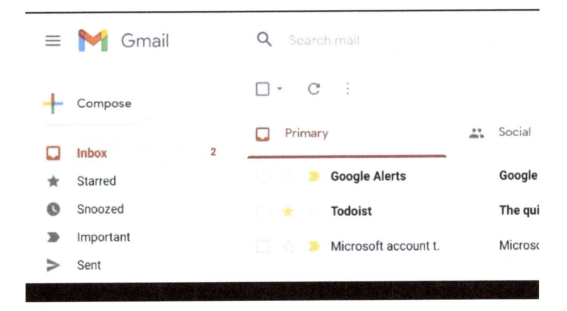

Setting Up Auto-Replies & Email Signatures

How to Set Up an Email Signature

A signature adds **professionalism** by including your **name, role, contact information, or company details**.

1. Click **Settings (⚙) → "See all settings"**.

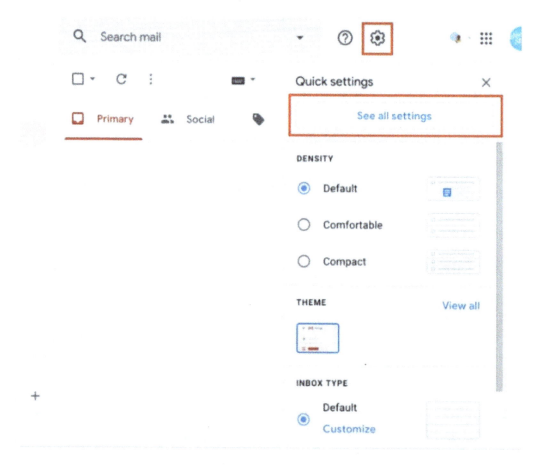

2. Scroll to the **"Signature"** section.
3. Click **"Create new"**, enter a signature name.

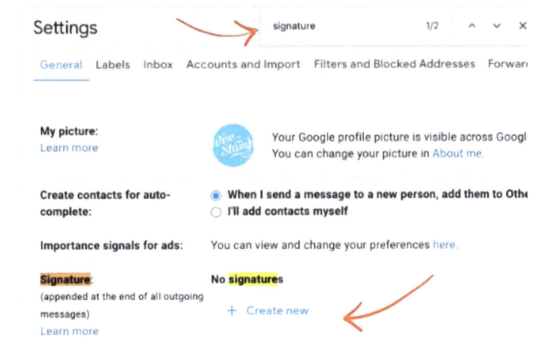

4. Type your signature, format it, and add images or links.
5. Click **"Save Changes"** at the bottom.

Setting Up Auto-Reply (Out-of-Office Response)

1. Go to **Settings (⚙) → "See all settings"**.

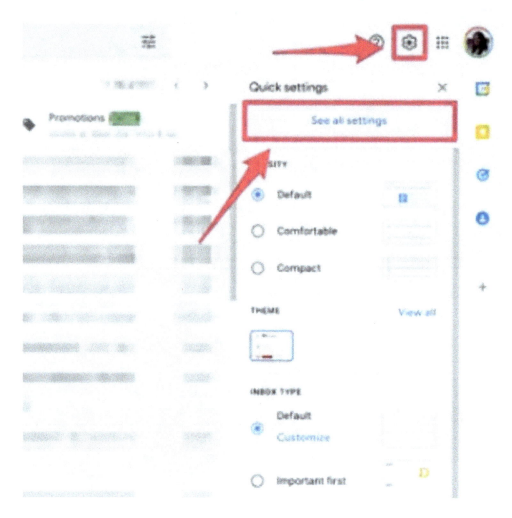

2. Scroll to **"Vacation Responder"**.
3. Toggle **ON** and set:
    o **Start & End Date**
    o **Subject & Message**
4. Click **"Save Changes"**.

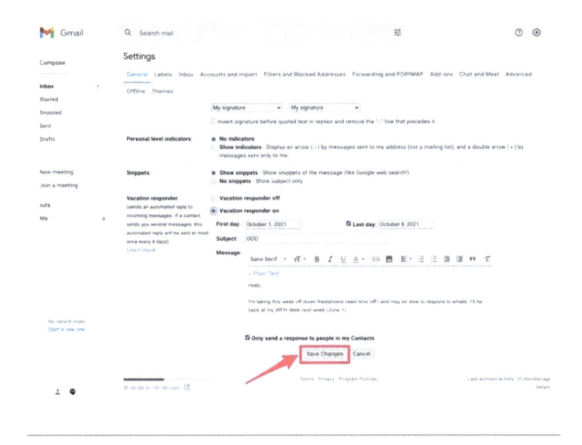

Using Gmail Shortcuts for Speed & Efficiency

Gmail offers keyboard shortcuts to **speed up email management**.

How to Enable Gmail Shortcuts

1. Go to **Settings (⚙)** → **"See all settings"**.
2. Scroll to **"Keyboard Shortcuts"** and toggle ON.
3. Click **"Save Changes"**.

Essential Gmail Shortcuts

Shortcut	Function
C	Compose new email
R	Reply to an email
F	Forward an email
Ctrl + Enter	Send email
E	Archive email
Shift + U	Mark as unread

Scheduling Emails for Later Delivery

Need to send an email at a specific time? Gmail lets you schedule it!

How to Schedule an Email

1. Click **"Compose"** and draft your email.
2. Click the **downward arrow (⯆) next to "Send"**.

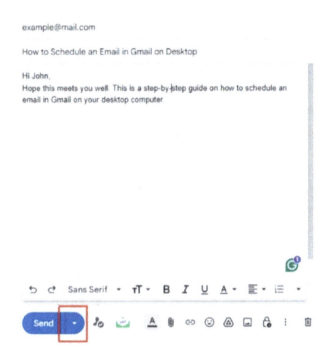

3. Select **"Schedule send"**.

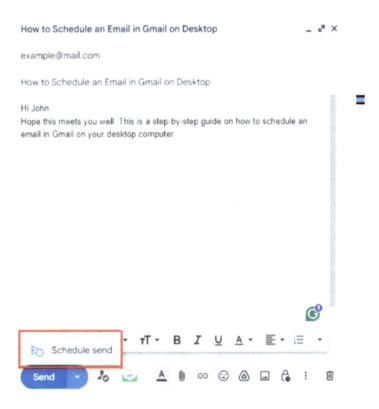

4. Choose a date and time.

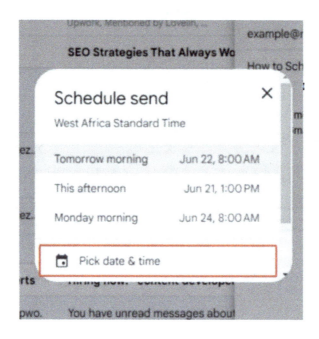

5. Click **"Schedule send"** to confirm.

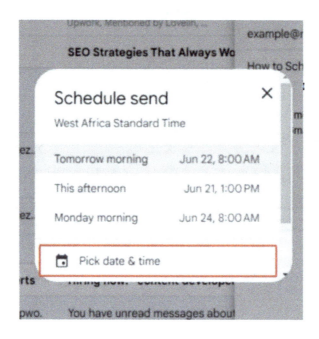

Your email will be sent automatically at the scheduled time.

Managing Spam & Unwanted Emails

Spam emails can **clutter your inbox and pose security risks**. Gmail automatically filters most spam, but you can take additional steps.

How to Mark an Email as Spam

1. Open the suspicious email.
2. Click the **three dots (⁝)** → **"Report spam"**.

How to Block a Sender

1. Open the email from the sender you want to block.
2. Click the **three dots (⁝)** → **"Block [Sender]"**.
3. Click **Confirm**.

Unsubscribing from Promotional Emails

1. Open a marketing email.
2. Click **"Unsubscribe"** (found near the sender's email address).

Chapter 5: Google Chat – Instant Messaging & Team Collaboration

---

I n today's fast-paced digital world, **quick and effective communication** is essential for personal and professional productivity. **Google Chat** is a powerful tool within Google Workspace that **simplifies messaging, enhances team collaboration, and integrates seamlessly with other Google services**.

This chapter will explore:

- The Google chat interface.
- Creating and managing conversations.
- Using group chats and spaces for teamwork.
- Sending files, links, and attachments.
- Integrating Google chat with Gmail.

Understanding Google Chat Interface

Google Chat provides a clean and **user-friendly layout** designed for **instant communication and collaboration**.

Accessing Google Chat

You can use Google Chat via:

- The **web app** at chat.google.com
- The **Gmail sidebar** (if enabled)
- The **Google Chat mobile app** (available on iOS & Android)

Exploring the Google Chat Dashboard

When you open Google Chat, you'll see:

1. **Navigation Panel (Left Sidebar)**
   - o **Chat**: Displays individual and group conversations.
   - o **Spaces**: Shows shared team workspaces.
   - o **Meet**: Shortcut to Google Meet video calls.
   - o **Search Bar**: Find messages, files, or contacts.
2. **Main Chat Window**
   - o Displays the active conversation.
   - o Includes a message input box and formatting options.
3. **Chat Settings (⚙ Icon in Gmail)**
   - o Customize notifications, theme, and integration settings.

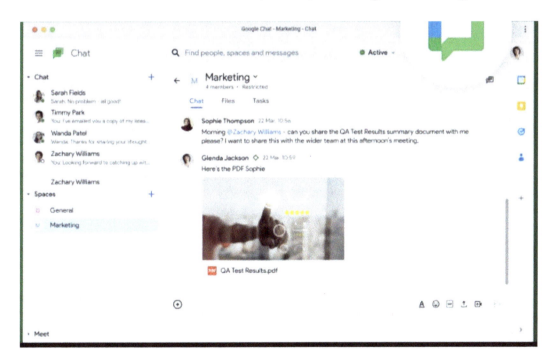

Creating & Managing Conversations

Google Chat supports **direct messages (DMs), group chats, and Spaces**.

Starting a New Conversation (One-on-One Chat)

1. Click the **"+" (Start a chat) button** in the left sidebar.

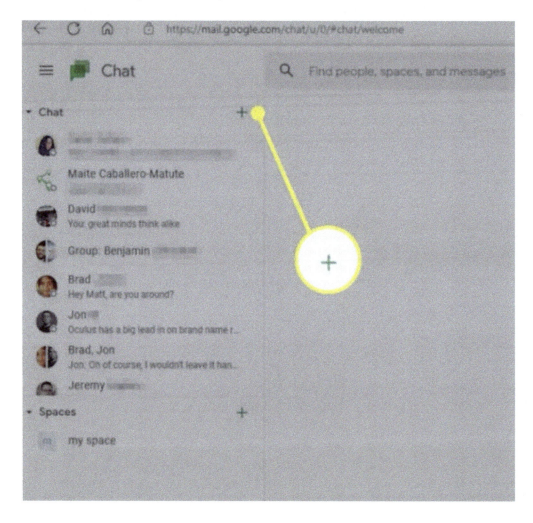

2. Select **"Message someone"** and enter the recipient's name or email.
3. Type your message and hit **Enter** to send.

Managing a Conversation

- **Edit a sent message**: Hover over the message → Click **Edit (━)**.
- **Delete a message**: Hover over the message → Click **Delete (🗑)**.
- **Pin important messages**: Click **More options (⏷)** → **Pin**.

Using Group Chats & Spaces for Team Collaboration

Group chats and Spaces enhance teamwork by allowing **multiple people to communicate in a shared space**.

Creating a Group Chat

1. Click **"+" (Start a chat)** → **"Create a group chat"**.
2. Add participants by entering their names or emails.
3. Click **"Start"** and begin chatting.

Key Features of Group Chats:

- **Name the chat** for easy identification.
- **React with emojis** to messages.
- **Share files and links** with the team.

Using Spaces for Team Collaboration

Google Spaces (formerly called Rooms) **enhance teamwork by allowing structured conversations, file sharing, and task assignments**.

How to Create a Space:

1. Click **"+" (Start a chat)** → **"Create a Space"**.

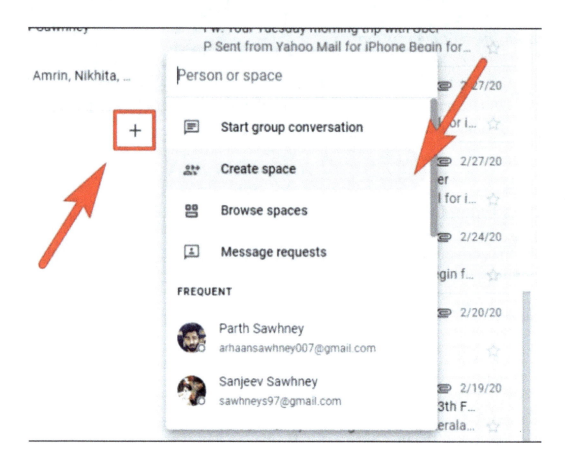

2. Enter a **name for the Space** (e.g., "Marketing Team" or "Project Alpha").
3. Add members by entering their emails.
4. Click **Create**, and the Space will appear in your chat list.

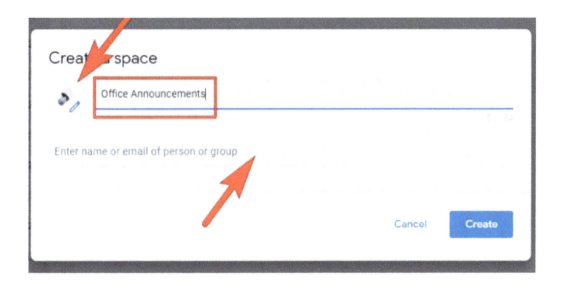

Key Features of Spaces:

- **Threaded conversations** keep discussions organized.
- **File sharing** allows easy collaboration.
- **Task assignments** help track progress.
- **@Mentions** notify specific team members.

Sending Files, Links, & Attachments

Google Chat allows users to **share documents, images, and links seamlessly**.

How to Send a File or Image in a Chat

1. Click the **paperclip 📎 (Attach) icon** in the message box.
2. Choose a file from your computer or Google Drive.
3. Click **Send (▷)**.

Sharing Google Drive Files in Google Chat

1. Click the **Google Drive icon** in the chat window.
2. Select a file from your Drive.

3. Adjust **permissions (View, Comment, or Edit)**.
4. Click **Insert** and send the file.

Sharing Links in Google Chat

- Paste any URL in the message box → Press **Enter**.
- Google Chat will automatically generate a **preview** (if supported).

Integrating Google Chat with Gmail

Google Chat is **seamlessly integrated into Gmail**, allowing users to **send and receive messages without leaving their inbox**.

How to Enable Google Chat in Gmail

1. Open **Gmail** and click **Settings (⚙) → See all settings**.
2. Go to the **"Chat and Meet"** tab.
3. Select **"Google Chat"** and click **Save Changes**.

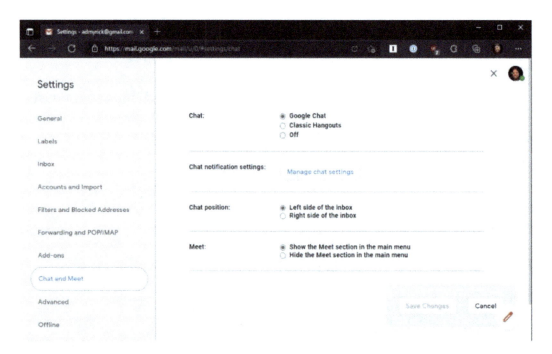

Using Google Chat in Gmail

Once enabled, a **Chat section** will appear in the Gmail sidebar.

- **Click a contact's name** to start a chat.
- **Use the search bar** to find old conversations.
- **Switch between emails and chats easily** without opening a new tab.

Chapter 6: Google Meet – Hosting & Managing Video Meetings

I n today's digital world, **video meetings have become essential** for remote work, education, and business collaboration. **Google Meet** is Google's official video conferencing tool, offering **secure, high-quality video calls** that integrate seamlessly with other Google Workspace tools.

This chapter will explore:

✓ **Setting up a Google Meet video call**

✓ **Inviting participants & managing permissions**

✓ **Using background effects & filters**

✓ **Sharing your screen & presenting slides**

✓ **Recording & saving meetings**

Setting Up a Google Meet Video Call

Google Meet allows users to **start or schedule video calls easily**, whether for team meetings, virtual events, or one-on-one discussions.

Method 1: Starting an Instant Meeting

To start a meeting immediately:

1. Open Google Meet.
2. Click **"New Meeting"**.
3. Choose **"Start an instant meeting"**.

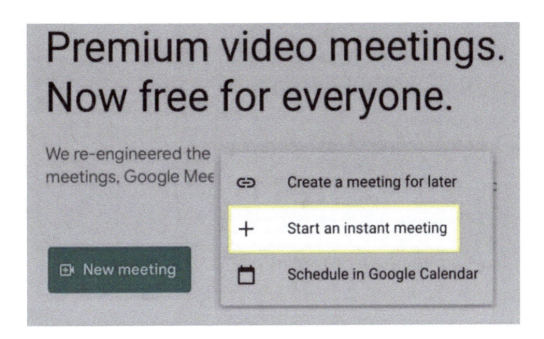

Premium video meetings. Now free for everyone.

We re-engineered the
meetings, Google Mee

🔗   Create a meeting for later

＋   Start an instant meeting

📅   Schedule in Google Calendar

⊞ New meeting

4. Google Meet will generate a **meeting link** and open the video call.
5. Click **"Copy joining info"** and send it to participants.

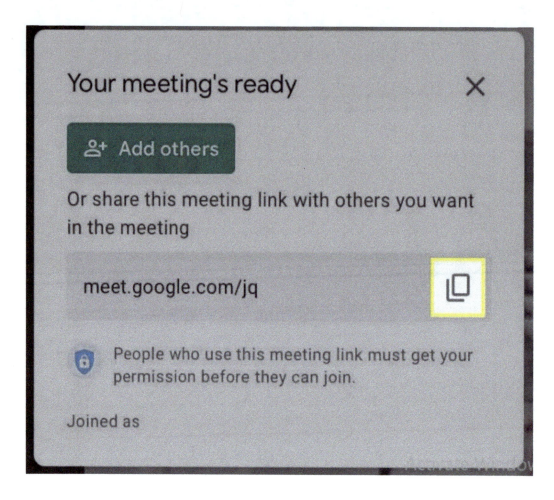

Method 2: Scheduling a Meeting in Google Calendar

For planned meetings, it's best to **schedule through Google Calendar**:

1. Open **Google Calendar** at <u>calendar.google.com</u>. Or from Google Meet, click "**New meeting**". Select "**Schedule in Google Calendar**".
2. Click "**Create**" → Select "**Event**".
3. Add a **title, date, and time**.
4. Click "**Add Google Meet video conferencing**".
5. Add participants by entering their email addresses.
6. Click **Save** → Select **Send invites** to notify attendees.

💡 *Tip: Scheduled meetings will automatically appear in Google Meet under "My Meetings."*

Inviting Participants & Managing Permissions

Once a meeting is created, you can **invite attendees and control access** to ensure a smooth experience.

Inviting Participants

You can invite people in three ways:
✓ **Share the meeting link**: Copy the link and send it via email, chat, or messaging apps.
✓ **Add participants directly**: Click **"People"** → Select **"Add people"** and enter email addresses.
✓ **Through Google Calendar**: If the meeting is scheduled, Google Calendar automatically sends invitations.

Managing Participant Permissions

As the host, you can **control access and interactions**:

Admitting or Denying Entry

- Participants who aren't invited must **request to join**.
- Click **"Admit"** to allow or **"Deny entry"** to block.

Muting Participants

- Click the **"People" tab**.
- Select a participant → Click **"Mute"** (◀◉ **icon)**.

Removing Participants

- Click **More options (⍰) next to a participant's name** → Select **"Remove"**.

Locking the Meeting (Host Controls)

- Click on the three dots (...) button

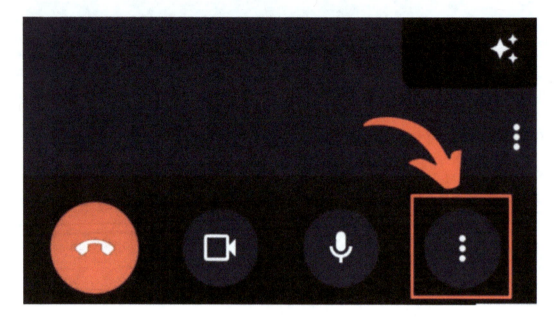

- Click **"Host controls"** → Toggle **"Quick Access"** OFF.

- This prevents uninvited users from joining.

Using Background Effects & Filters

Google Meet offers **virtual backgrounds, blur effects, and filters** to enhance privacy and improve the video experience.

Changing Your Background Before a Meeting

1. Open **Google Meet** and start a meeting.
2. Click on the three dots (...) button.

3. Click **Apply visual effects**

4. Choose from:

    ✓ **Blur Background** (Slight blur or full blur)

    ✓ **Pre-set Backgrounds** (Office, nature, cityscapes, etc.)

    ✓ **Upload Your Own Image**

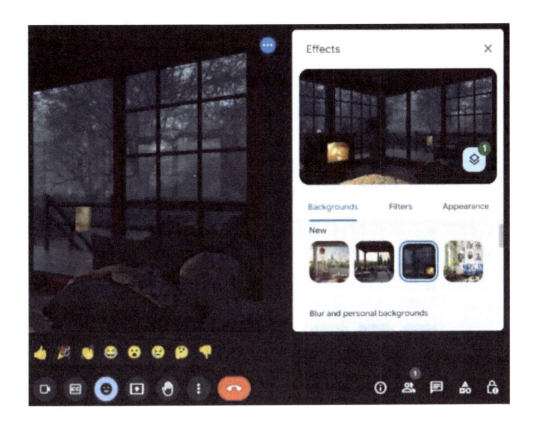

Applying Effects During a Meeting

1. Click **More options (⏷)** → **Apply visual effects**.
2. Select a **background, filter, or blur effect**.

💡 *Tip: Blurred backgrounds can help reduce distractions in professional meetings!*

Sharing Your Screen & Presenting Slides

Screen sharing allows you to **show documents, presentations, or webpages** during a meeting.

How to Share Your Screen in Google Meet

1. Click **"Present now" (🖥 icon) at the bottom of the screen**.

2. Choose from:

✓ **Your Entire Screen** (Shares everything on your display)

✓ **A Window** (Shares a specific app or browser window)

✓ **A Chrome Tab** (Best for sharing audio and videos)

3. Click **"Share"** to start presenting.

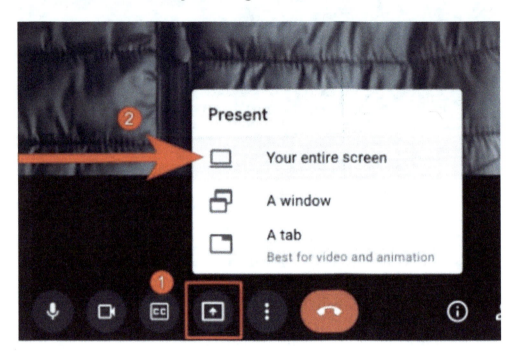

Presenting Google Slides in a Meeting

1. Open your Google Slides presentation.
2. Click **"Slideshow"** drop-down button. Select **Presenter view.**

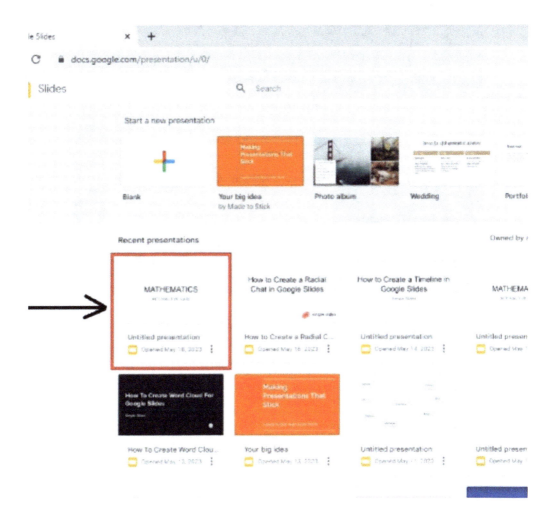

3. Go back to Google Meet → Click **"Present now"** → Select **"A Window"**.

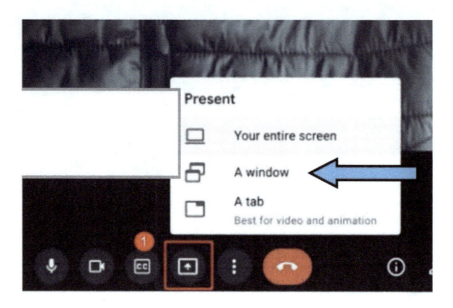

4. Choose the **Google Slides window** and click **"Share"**.

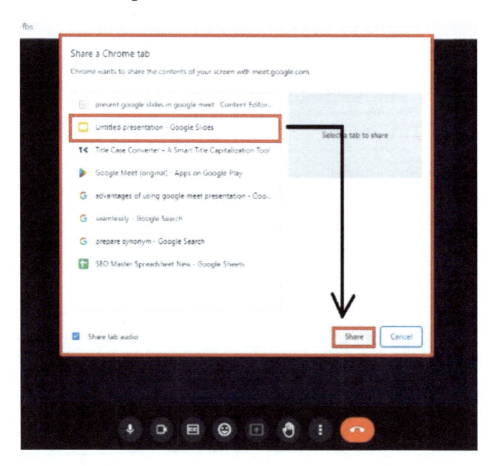

MATHEMATICS

INTERACTIVE QUIZ

💡 *Tip: Use the "Presenter View" in Google Slides to see speaker notes privately while presenting!*

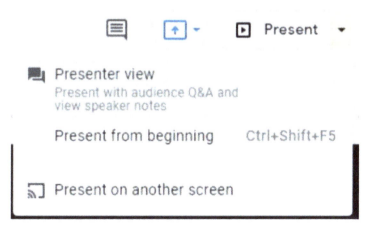

Recording & Saving Meetings

Recording a meeting allows participants to **review discussions later**, making it useful for training sessions, presentations, and important meetings.

How to Record a Google Meet Meeting

1. Click on the three dots button (...) → **"Record meeting"**.
2. A **notification will inform all participants** that recording has started.
3. To **stop recording**, click the three dots button (...) → **"Stop recording"**.

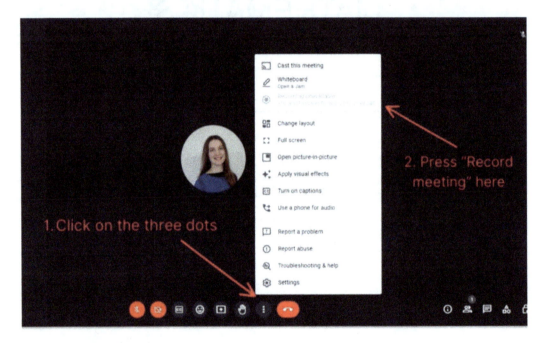

Where Are Google Meet Recordings Saved?

✓ Recordings are automatically **saved to Google Drive** (under "Meet Recordings" in the host's Drive).

✓ Google will send an **email with the recording link**.

✓ Hosts can **share, download, or delete the recording** from Drive.

◆ *Recording is only available for Google Workspace paid plans.*

PART 3: Productivity & File Management

Chapter 7: Google Drive – Storing, Organizing & Sharing Files

Google Drive is a **powerful cloud storage platform** that allows you to store, organize, and share files from anywhere. Whether you're managing personal documents, team projects, or business files, Google Drive provides **secure, accessible, and collaborative storage solutions**.

This chapter will cover:

✓ **Uploading & Downloading Files in Google Drive**

✓ **Creating & Organizing Folders**

✓ **Sharing Files with Different Access Levels**

✓ **Collaborating on Shared Files**

✓ **Managing File Versions & Restoring Older Versions**

✓ **Google Drive Keyboard Shortcuts**

Uploading & Downloading Files in Google Drive

How to Upload Files to Google Drive

Google Drive allows you to **store files of any format**, including documents, images, videos, PDFs, and spreadsheets.

Method 1: Uploading via the Web Browser

1. Open Google Drive.
2. Click **"+ New"** (on the left panel).

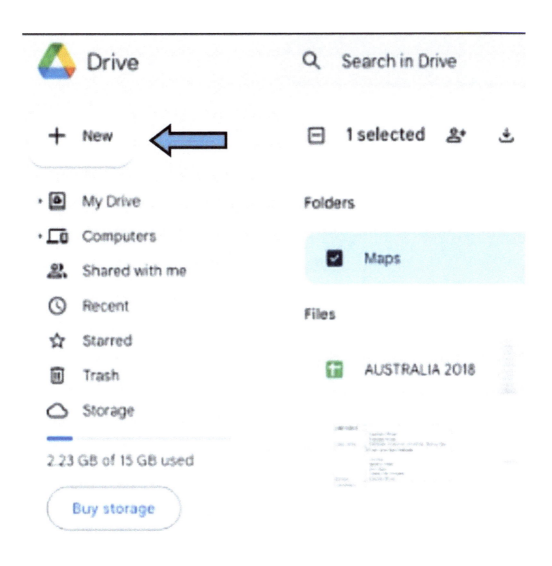

3. Select **"File upload"** or **"Folder upload"**.

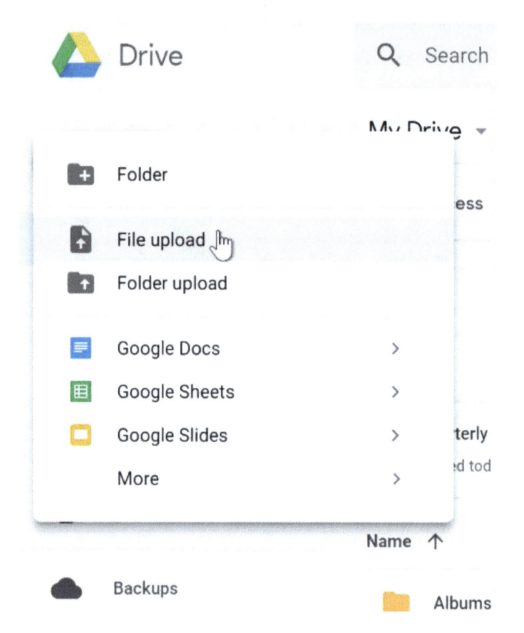

4. Choose the file or folder from your computer and click **Open**.
5. The file will start uploading, and a **progress bar** will appear at the bottom.

Method 2: Drag-and-Drop Upload

1. Open **Google Drive** in a browser.
2. Open **your computer's file explorer**.

3. **Drag the file** from your computer and **drop it** into Google Drive.

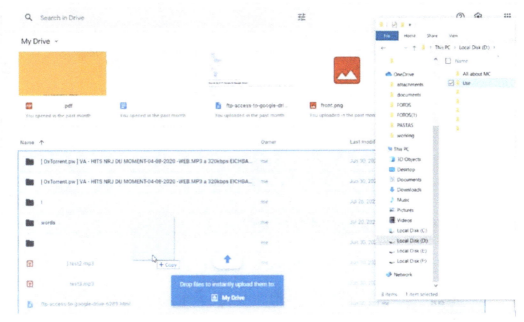

Drag and Drop Files from PC to Google Drive

💡 *Tip: Upload speeds depend on your internet connection. Large files may take longer to process.*

How to Download Files from Google Drive

Method 1: Downloading Individual Files

1. Open **Google Drive**.
2. Right-click on the file.
3. Select **"Download"**.
4. The file will be saved to your computer's default download location.

Method 2: Downloading Multiple Files or Folders

1. Hold down **Ctrl (Windows) / Cmd (Mac)** and select multiple files.
2. Right-click and select **"Download"**.

3. Google Drive will **compress the files into a ZIP folder** before downloading.

💡 *Tip: If you need to download an entire Google Docs or Sheets file, convert it to a PDF or Microsoft format before downloading.*

Creating & Organizing Folders

A well-structured folder system **makes file management easier**.

How to Create Folders in Google Drive

1. Click **"+ New"** in Google Drive.
2. Select **"Folder"**.

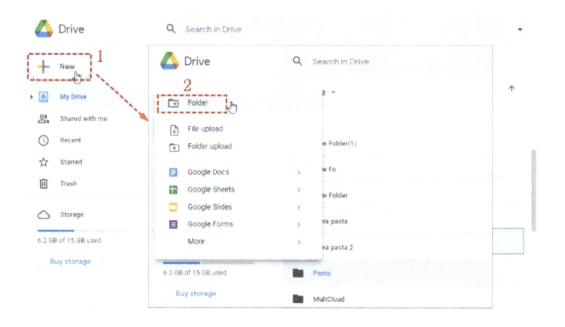

3. Enter a **folder name** and click **"Create"**.

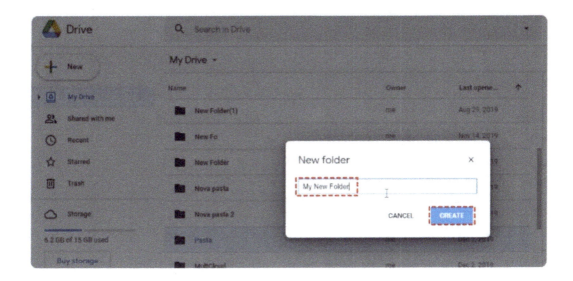

Organizing Files with Folders

✓ **Move files into folders**: Drag and drop files into folders.

✓ **Use color coding**: Right-click a folder → Select **"Change color"** → Pick a color.

✓ **Use a naming system**: Keep file names **descriptive and consistent** (e.g., "Invoices_2024_Q1").

💡 *Tip: Google Drive automatically sorts files by last modified date, but you can manually arrange them using folders.*

Sharing Files with Different Access Levels

Google Drive makes **file sharing easy**, with different permission settings.

How to Share Files or Folders

1. **Right-click** the file or folder.
2. Select **"Share"**.

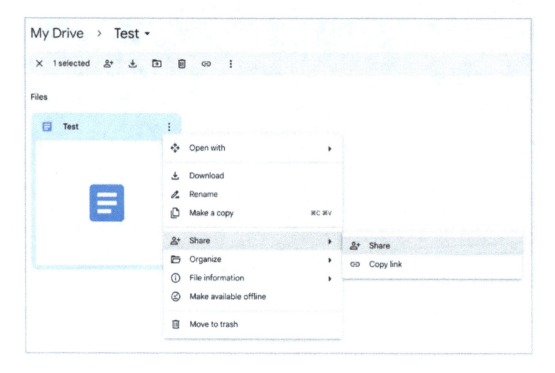

3. Enter the **email addresses** of people you want to share with.
4. Click the **drop-down menu** to set permissions:

    ✓ **Viewer** – Can only view the file.

    ✓ **Commenter** – Can add comments but not edit.

    ✓ **Editor** – Can make changes to the file.

5. Click **"Send"** to share.

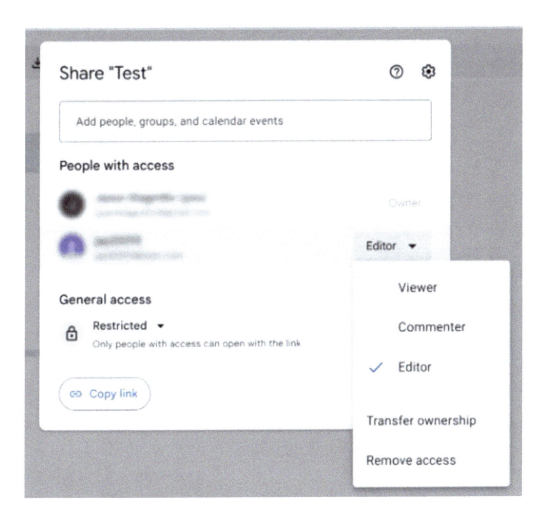

Generating a Shareable Link

1. Right-click the file → Select **"Share"**.
2. Click **"Copy link"**.

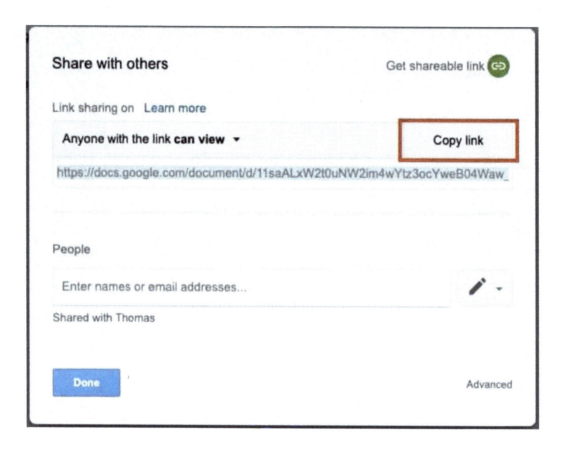

3. Change access settings:

   ✓ **Restricted** – Only invited people can access.

   ✓ **Anyone with the link** – Anyone with the link can view, comment, or edit.

4. Copy and share the link.

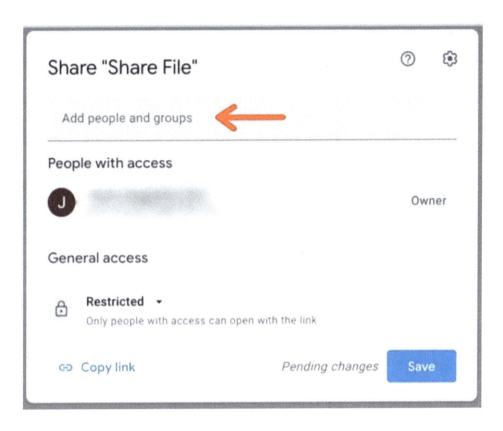

💡 *Tip: Always review permissions before sharing sensitive files!*

Collaborating on Shared Files

Google Drive allows **real-time collaboration** in **Docs, Sheets, and Slides**.

How to Work on a Shared File

✓ **Make live edits**: Changes appear instantly for all users.

✓ **Add comments**: Highlight text → Click **"Comment"** → Type a message.

✓ **View version history**: Click **"File"** → **"Version history"** to see previous edits.

✓ **Assign tasks**: In comments, type **"@"** followed by a teammate's email.

💡 *Tip: Use the "Suggesting" mode in Google Docs to make edits without changing the original text.*

Managing File Versions & Restoring Older Versions

Google Drive **automatically saves file versions**, allowing you to recover previous edits.

How to View & Restore Previous Versions

1. Open a Google Docs, Sheets, or Slides file.
2. Click **"File"** → **"Version history"** → **"See version history"**.
3. On the right panel, view past versions with timestamps.
4. Click a version and select **"Restore this version"** to revert.

Managing File Versions for Uploaded Files (e.g., PDFs, Images, Videos)

1. Right-click the uploaded file.
2. Select **"Manage versions"**.
3. Click **"Upload new version"** to replace the file without changing the link.
4. Click **"Keep forever"** to prevent automatic deletion of old versions.

💡 *Tip: Google Drive keeps past versions for 30 days or up to 100 versions, whichever comes first.*

Google Drive Keyboard Shortcuts

Using keyboard shortcuts can **save time** and improve workflow.

Action	Shortcut (Windows & Mac)
Create a new folder	Shift + F
Upload a file	U
Open file preview	P
Rename a file	N
Select multiple files	Shift + Click
Search Google Drive	/
Open sharing settings	.
Delete a file	Delete

💡 *Tip: Press "Shift + ?" in Google Drive to view all shortcuts.*

Chapter 8: Google Docs – Creating & Editing Documents

G oogle Docs is a **powerful online word processor** that allows you to create, edit, and collaborate on documents in real time. Whether you're drafting a report, writing an article, or working on a group project, Google Docs provides **a seamless and efficient writing experience**.

This chapter will cover:
- Navigating Google Docs Interface
- Formatting Text, Paragraphs, & Styles
- Inserting Images, Tables, Links & Footnotes
- Collaborating with Others Using Comments & Suggestions
- Using Voice Typing & Add-ons

Navigating Google Docs Interface

Google Docs has an **intuitive layout** similar to traditional word processors like Microsoft Word.

Key Components of the Interface

- **Toolbar** – Provides formatting options (bold, italic, font size, etc.).
- **Menu Bar** – Contains advanced features like file export, page setup, and extensions.
- **Document Area** – Where you type and edit text.
- **Sidebar** – Used for comments, document outline, and add-ons.

Tip: Press "Ctrl + /" (Windows) or "Cmd + /" (Mac) to quickly search for any tool in Google Docs.

Formatting Text, Paragraphs, & Styles

Consistent formatting improves readability and document structure.

Basic Text Formatting

- **Bold** – Select text → Click **B** or press **Ctrl + B**.
- **Italic** – Select text → Click **I** or press **Ctrl + I**.
- **Underline** – Select text → Click **U** or press **Ctrl + U**.

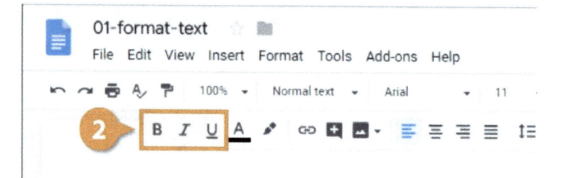

Font & Size – Change from the toolbar dropdown.

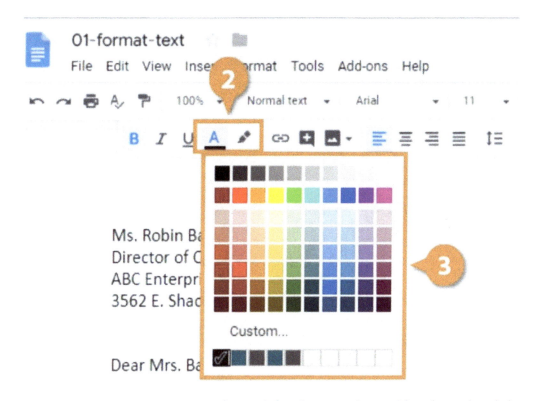

Paragraph Formatting

● **Line Spacing** – Click **Format** → **Line & paragraph spacing** → Choose spacing.
● **Alignment** – Select text → Click **Left, Center, Right, or Justify** icons.
● **Bulleted & Numbered Lists** – Click **Bulleted list** or **Numbered list** icons in the toolbar.

Applying Text Styles (Headings & Subheadings)

● Click the **Styles dropdown** (next to font selection).
● Choose **Title, Heading 1, Heading 2, etc.** to structure your document.

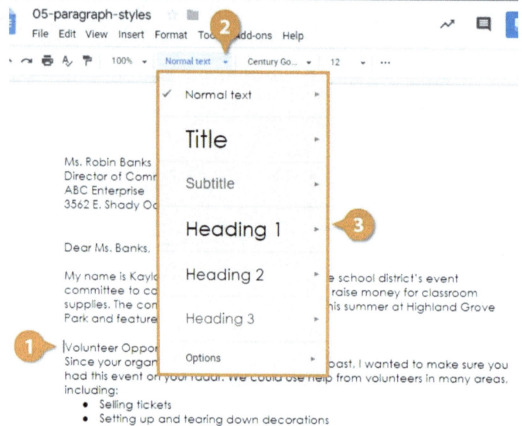

💡 *Tip: Using "Headings" helps generate an automatic **Table of Contents**.*

Inserting Images, Tables, Links & Footnotes

How to Insert an Image

● Click **"Insert"** → **"Image"**.
● Choose from **Upload, Google Drive, Web Search, or Camera.**

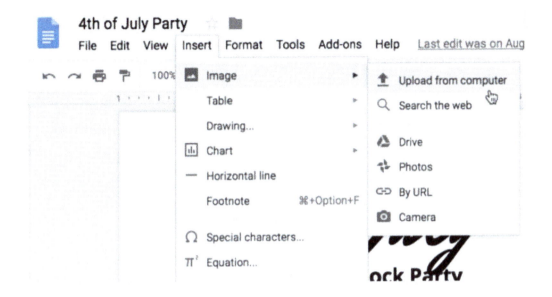

How to Insert a Table

● Click **"Insert"** → **"Table"** → Select rows & columns.

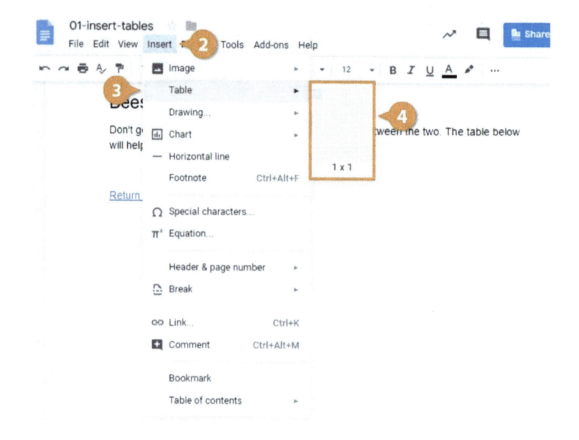

● Use the **Table properties** option to adjust color, alignment, and borders.

Adding Links (Hyperlinks)

● Highlight text → Click **"Insert"** → **"Link"** or press **Ctrl + K**.
● Enter the **URL** and click **Apply**.

Adding Footnotes

● Click where you want the footnote.
● Click **"Insert"** → **"Footnote"**.
● Type the reference or citation at the bottom of the page.

💡 *Tip: Right-click an image to access "Image Options" and adjust brightness, contrast, or wrap text around it.*

Collaborating with Others Using Comments & Suggestions

Google Docs enables **real-time collaboration**, making teamwork seamless.

Adding Comments

● Highlight text → Click the **comment icon** or press **Ctrl + Alt + M**.

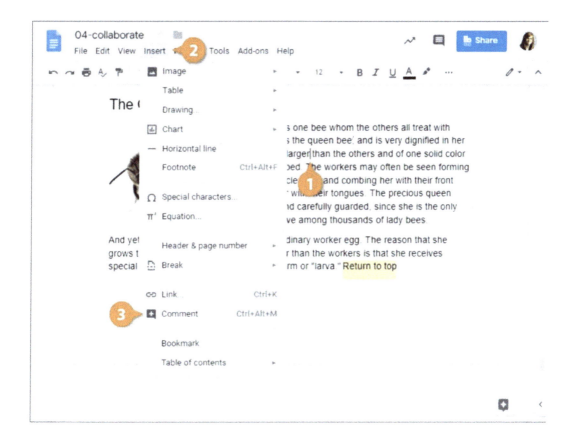

● Type your comment and click **Comment**.

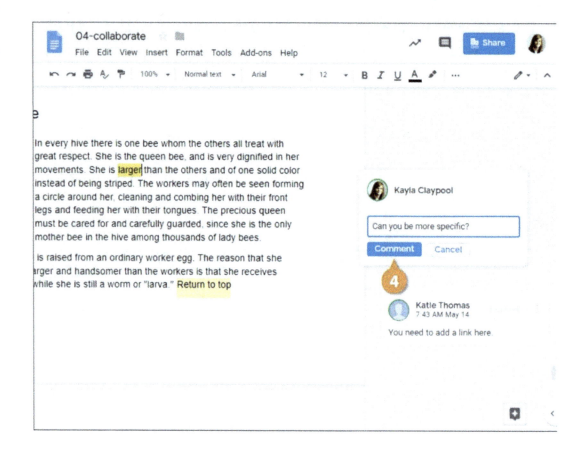

Suggesting Edits (Track Changes Mode)

● Click **Editing mode (pencil icon)** → **Suggesting**.

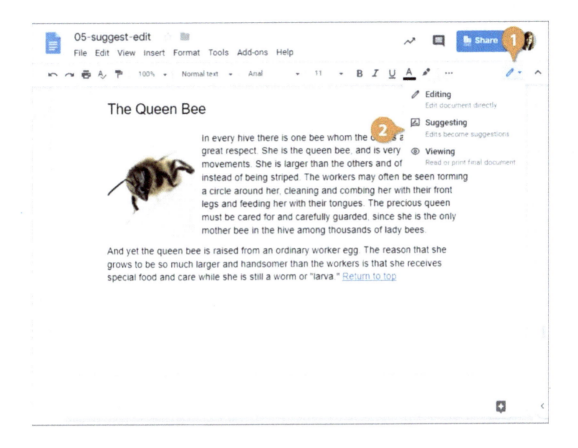

● Any changes will appear as suggestions instead of direct edits.
● Click **"Accept" or "Reject"** to apply or discard suggestions.

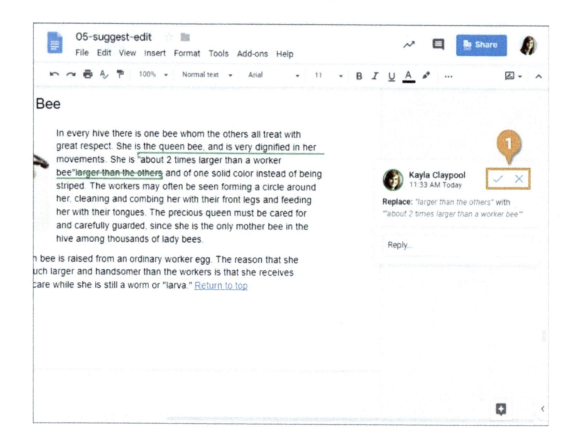

Assigning Tasks in Comments

● Type **@ followed by an email** to assign a task (e.g., @JohnDoe).
● The person will receive an email notification.

💡 *Tip: Use "Version History"* **(File → Version History)** *to track and restore past document versions.*

Using Voice Typing & Add-ons

Google Docs offers **advanced tools** like voice typing and third-party add-ons.

How to Use Voice Typing

- Click **Tools → Voice Typing**.
- Click the **microphone icon** and start speaking.
- Click the microphone again to stop.

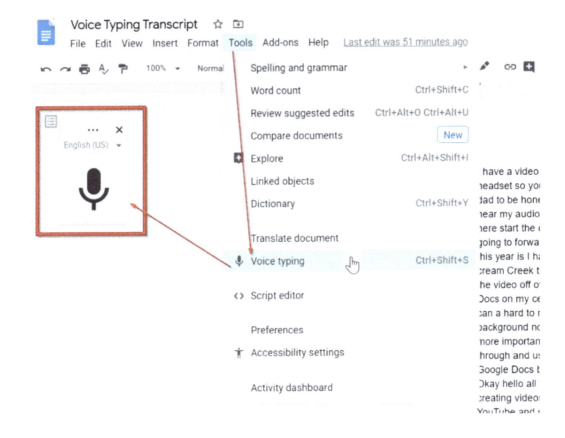

💡 *Tip: Use voice commands like "Period" or "New paragraph" for better control over formatting.*

Enhancing Docs with Add-ons

- Click **Extensions → Add-ons → Get add-ons**.
- Search for tools like:
- **Grammarly** – Improves spelling & grammar.
- **Doc Tools** – Enhances text formatting.
- **Table of Contents** – Auto-generates a clickable table of contents.

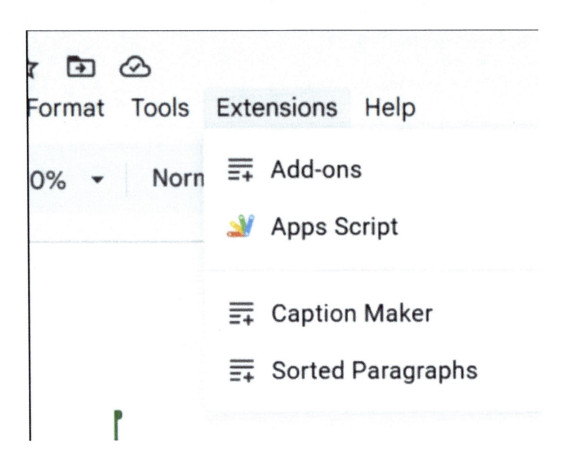

💡 *Tip: Add-ons help automate tasks and extend Google Docs' functionality.*

Chapter 9: Google Sheets – Mastering Spreadsheets

G oogle Sheets is a **powerful online spreadsheet tool** that allows users to organize, analyze, and visualize data efficiently. It provides real-time collaboration, automation features, and a wide range of functions to simplify data management.

This chapter will cover:
• **Basic Spreadsheet Navigation & Formatting**
• **Using Formulas & Functions (SUM, AVERAGE, VLOOKUP, etc.)**
• **Creating Charts & Graphs for Data Visualization**
• **Collaborating with Team Members in Google Sheets**
• **Automating Tasks with Google Sheets Macros**

Basic Spreadsheet Navigation & Formatting

Understanding the Google Sheets Interface

Google Sheets has a **structured layout** similar to Excel, consisting of:
• **Cells** – The building blocks of the spreadsheet (organized into rows and columns).
• **Rows & Columns** – Rows are numbered (1, 2, 3…), while columns are labeled (A, B, C…).
• **Formula Bar** – Displays content and formulas of selected cells.
• **Toolbar & Menus** – Provides formatting, sorting, and data analysis tools.

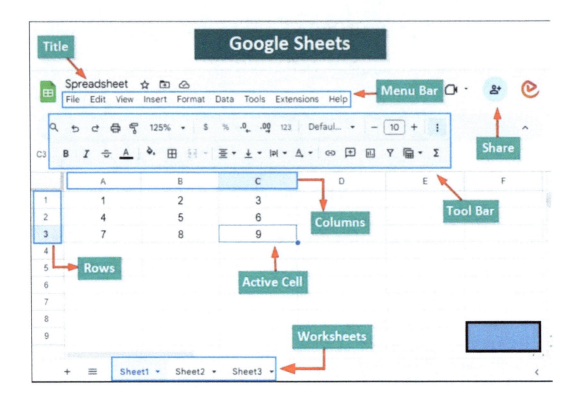

Formatting Cells for Readability

- **Change Font & Size** – Select the cell → Click the **font dropdown** → Choose style/size.
- **Cell Color & Borders** – Select the cell → Click the **paint bucket icon** for color or **border tool** for gridlines.

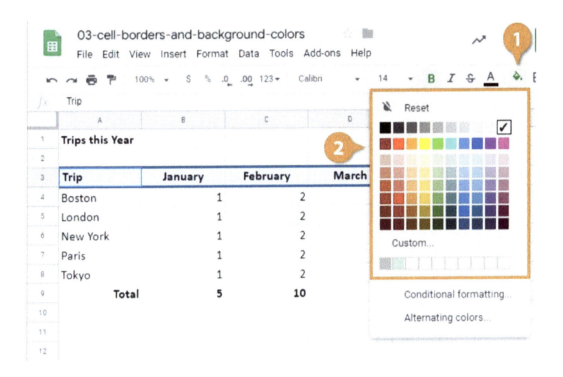

- **Text Alignment** – Select the cell → Click the **alignment tool** to center, left, or right-align text.
- **Number Formatting** – Click **Format** → **Number** to apply currency, date, or percentage formats.

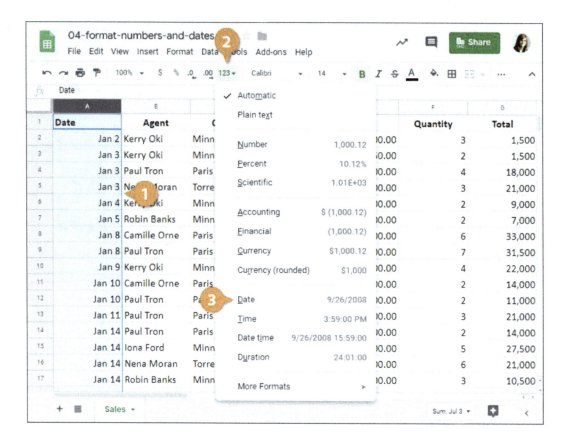

💡 *Tip: Use "Merge Cells" (Format → Merge) to create larger headers for improved readability.*

Using Formulas & Functions (SUM, AVERAGE, VLOOKUP, etc.)

Google Sheets offers **powerful built-in functions** to perform calculations and automate data processing.

Basic Formulas Every User Should Know

- **SUM** – Adds up values in a range. =SUM(E2:E4) (Adds values from E2 to E4).

E5   *fx*   =SUM(E2:E4)

	A	B	C	D	E
1	Trainers	Pokeball	Great Balls	Ultra Balls	
2	Iva		2	3	1	6
3	Liam		5	5	2	12
4	Adora		10	2	3	15
5					=SUM(E2:E4)

E6   *fx*

	A	B	C	D	E
1	Trainers	Pokeball	Great Balls	Ultra Balls	
2	Iva		2	3	1	6
3	Liam		5	5	2	12
4	Adora		10	2	3	15
5					33
6					
7					

- **AVERAGE** – Calculates the mean of a range. =AVERAGE(B1:B10) (Finds the average of B1 to B10).

- **IF** – Creates conditional logic. =IF(A1>50, "Pass", "Fail") (Checks if A1 is greater than 50).

Advanced Functions for Data Analysis

- **VLOOKUP** – Searches for a value in a column and returns related data. =VLOOKUP(101, A2:C10, 2, FALSE) (Finds 101 in column A and returns a value from column 2).
- **HLOOKUP** – Similar to VLOOKUP but searches horizontally.
- **COUNTIF** – Counts cells that meet a condition. =COUNTIF(A1:A10, ">50") (Counts how many cells in A1:A10 are greater than 50).

- **CONCATENATE** – Joins text from multiple cells. =CONCATENATE(A1, " ", B1) (Combines A1 and B1 with a space).

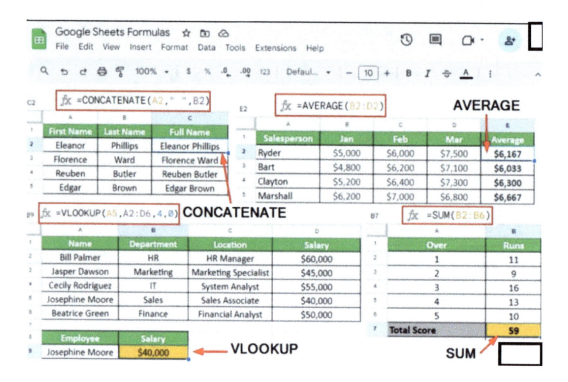

💡 Tip: *Start any formula with "=" and use **Tab** to autocomplete functions for faster input.*

Creating Charts & Graphs for Data Visualization

Charts and graphs **help transform raw data into meaningful insights**.

Steps to Create a Chart in Google Sheets

1. **Select the Data** – Highlight the cells that contain the data you want to visualize.
2. **Insert Chart** – Click **Insert → Chart** from the menu.

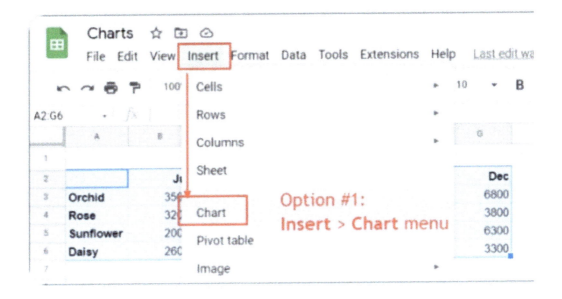

3. **Choose a Chart Type** – In the "Chart Editor" panel, select from:
   - **Bar Chart** – Best for comparing values.
   - **Pie Chart** – Shows percentage breakdowns.
   - **Line Chart** – Ideal for trends over time.

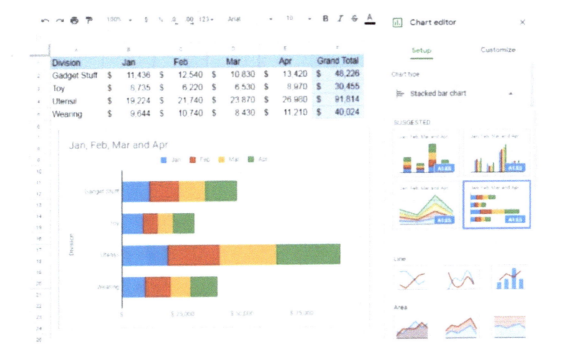

4. **Customize Chart Appearance** – Adjust colors, labels, and data series in the "Customize" tab.
5. **Move or Resize Chart** – Drag and drop the chart to position it anywhere in your sheet.

💡 *Tip: Use the "Trendline" feature in **Customize → Series** to analyze patterns in your data.*

Collaborating with Team Members in Google Sheets

Google Sheets allows **multiple users to work on the same spreadsheet simultaneously**.

How to Share a Google Sheet

1. Click the **"Share" button** in the top-right corner.

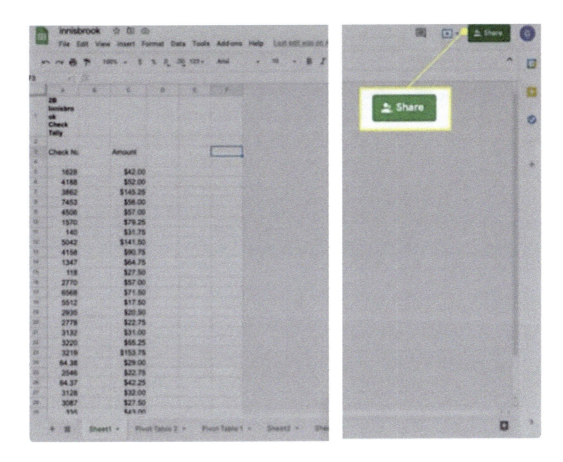

2. Enter **email addresses** of collaborators.

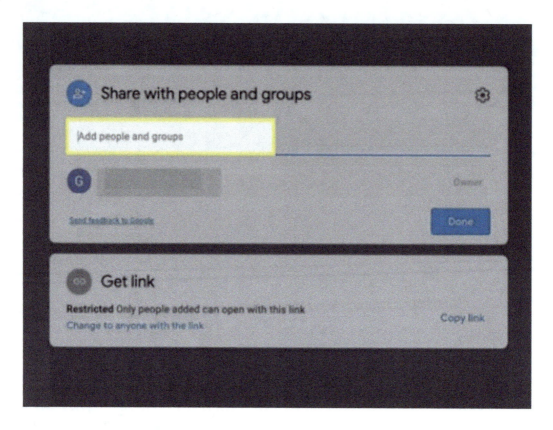

3. Set **permissions**:
   - **Viewer** – Can only view.
   - **Commenter** – Can leave comments but not edit.
   - **Editor** – Can fully edit the sheet.
4. Click **Send** to invite collaborators.

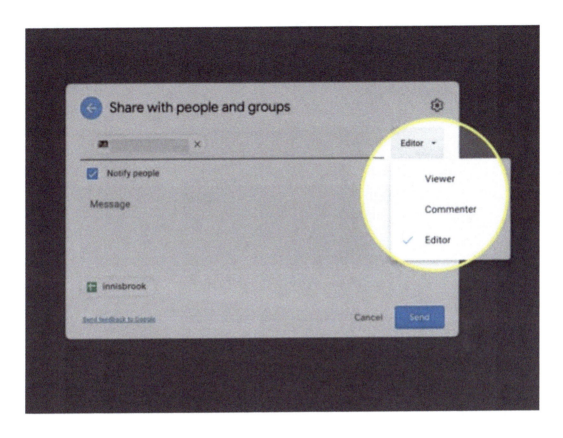

Adding & Resolving Comments

• Select a cell → Click **Comment icon** at the top of the screen or press **Ctrl + Alt + M**. Alternatively, you can right-click on a selected cell and select **Comment**.

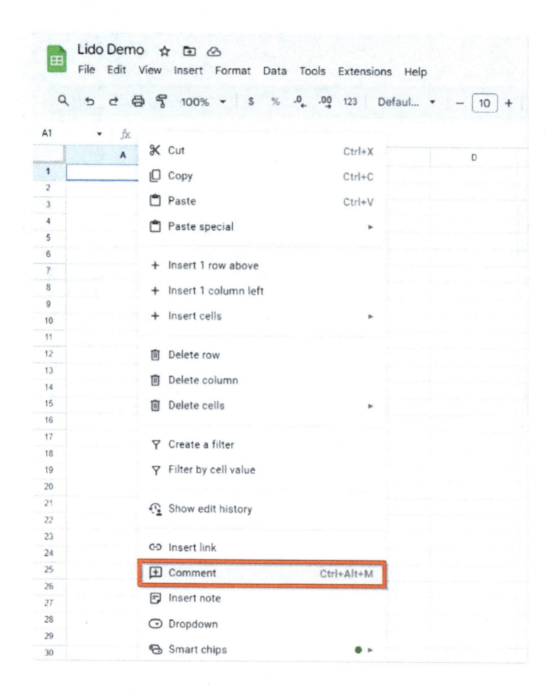

• Type a comment and click **Comment**.

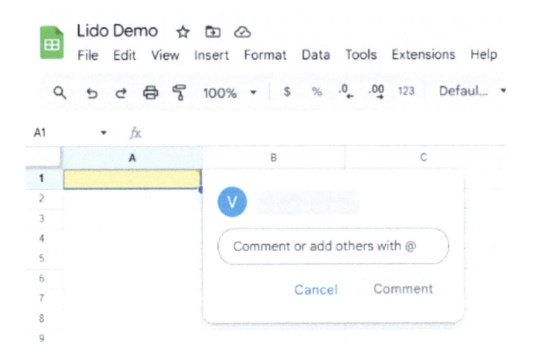

• Assign comments to specific users using @mention.

• Click **Resolve** when a comment is addressed.

💡 *Tip: Use "Version History" (**File → Version History**) to track and restore changes made by collaborators.*

Automating Tasks with Google Sheets Macros

Macros allow users to **record repetitive tasks** and **automate them with a single click**.

How to Create a Macro in Google Sheets

1. Click **Extensions → Macros → Record Macro**.

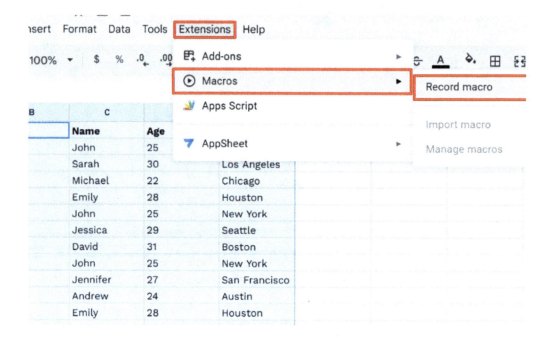

2. Perform the actions you want to automate (e.g., formatting, calculations).

3. Click **Save** and name your macro.

4. Assign a **keyboard shortcut** for quick execution. Go to Extensions>Macros>Manage macros

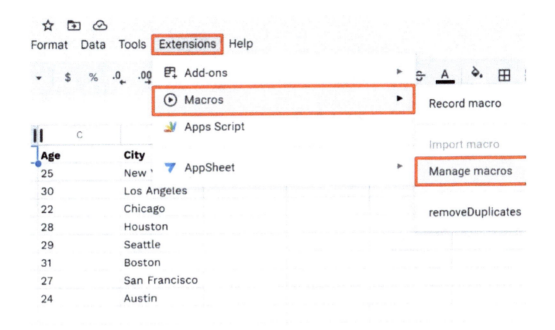

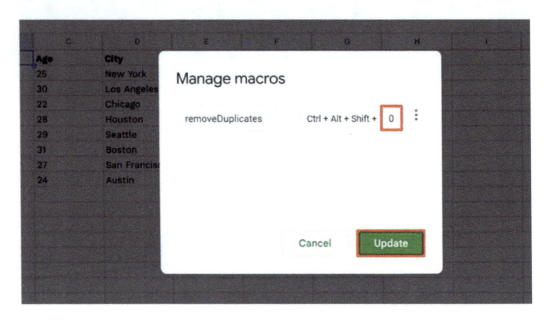

To run your macro, press `Ctrl` + `Alt` + `Shift` + `[your chosen digit]` on your keyboard. If you're using Google Sheets on Mac, use this key combo instead: `⌘` + `Option` + `Shift` + `[your chosen digit]`.

Click "Continue" when asked to authorize.

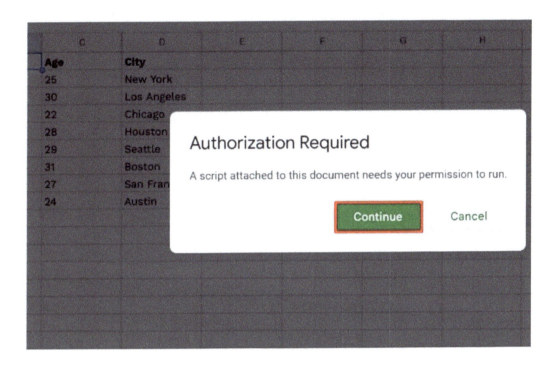

Choose your account, and click "Allow."

This will allow

Recorded Macros (Working With Macros) to:

● View and manage spreadsheets that this
application has been installed in

Make sure you trust Recorded Macros (Working With Macros)

You may be sharing sensitive info with this site or app. You can always see or remove access in your Google Account.

Learn how Google helps you share data safely.

See Recorded Macros (Working With Macros)'s Privacy Policy and Terms of Service.

Cancel   Allow

5. Run the macro anytime by clicking **Extensions → Macros → Your Macro Name**. or by using the keyboard shortcut you just created.

Using Google Apps Script for Advanced Automation

Google Apps Script lets users write JavaScript-based scripts to automate tasks.

Example: A script to **automatically send email reminders** based on spreadsheet data.

```javascript
function sendReminders() {
  var sheet = SpreadsheetApp.getActiveSpreadsheet().getSheetByName("Reminders");
  var data = sheet.getDataRange().getValues();

  for (var i = 1; i < data.length; i++) {
    var email = data[i][1]; // Email column
    var message = "Reminder: " + data[i][2]; // Message column

    MailApp.sendEmail(email, "Task Reminder", message);
  }
}
```

💡 Tip: Use "**Apps Script Editor**" (Extensions → Apps Script) to create and run custom automation scripts.

Chapter 10: Google Slides – Designing Powerful Presentations

Google Slides is a **web-based presentation tool** that allows users to create, edit, and collaborate on slideshows for business, education, or personal use. It offers **easy-to-use design features**, real-time collaboration, and **cloud storage** for access from anywhere. In this chapter, we'll guide you step by step through the process of creating engaging presentations.

Creating a New Presentation from Scratch

Before diving into the features of Google Slides, it's important to understand the **basic steps** for creating a new presentation.

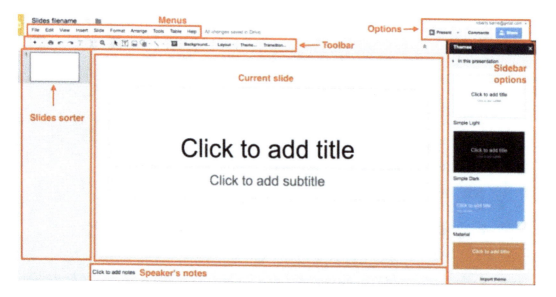

Step-by-Step Instructions for Creating a Presentation

1. **Open Google Slides**
   - Go to **slides.google.com**.
   - Select the names field at the top left corner and enter a new name. Select enter.

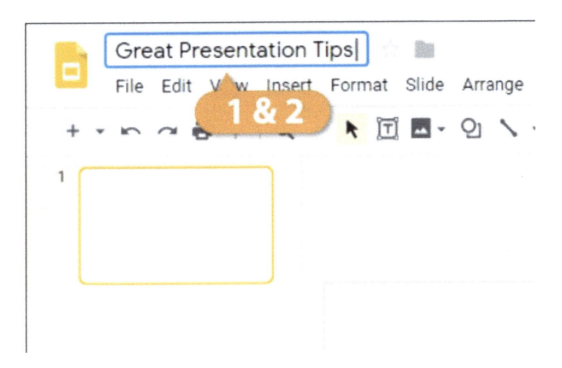

Another option is to Click **Blank** to start a new presentation from scratch or choose from a variety of templates available in the **Template Gallery**.

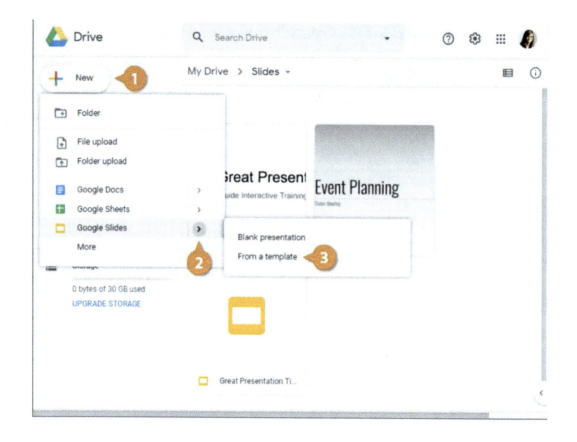

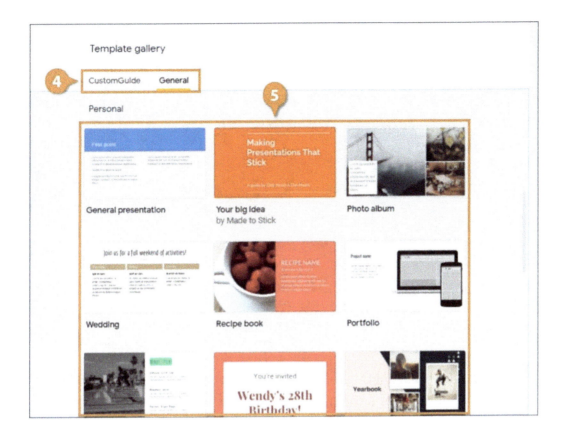

2. **Choosing a Theme**
   ○ Once your presentation is open, click **Slide → Change Theme** from the top menu.

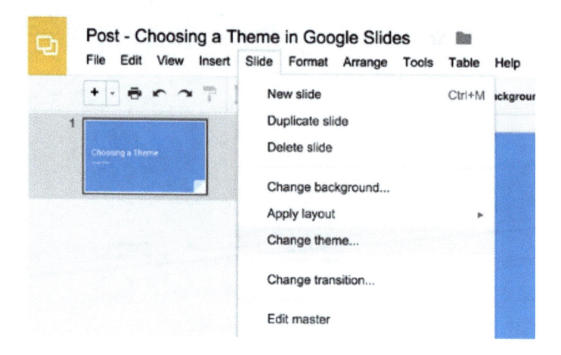

- o Choose from the default themes or click **Import Theme** to bring in your own or a theme from Google Drive.

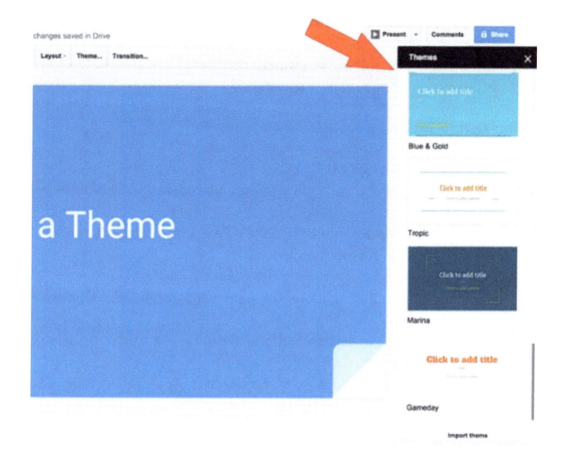

3. **Adding New Slides**
   o To add a new slide, click **Slide → New Slide** or press **Ctrl + M** (Cmd + M on Mac).
   o You can choose from different layouts such as Title Slide, Title and Content, Section Header, etc.
4. **Saving Your Presentation**
   o Google Slides automatically saves your work to **Google Drive**. You can also manually rename your presentation by clicking on the title at the top.

💡 *Tip: Use the "**Explore**" button in the bottom right to find layout suggestions and design ideas.*

Adding & Formatting Text, Images, and Videos

Designing a slide involves **adding multimedia elements** to engage your audience and make the presentation visually appealing.

Adding Text to Slides

1. **Click to Add Title or Text**
    - Select a text box or click on any placeholder text area to begin typing.
    - To add new text, go to **Insert → Text box**, then click and drag to draw a text box on the slide.
2. **Formatting Text**
    - Use the toolbar options to change **font style, size, color, and alignment**.
    - Bold, italics, underline, and color buttons are available to make your text stand out.
    - Highlight text and adjust **line spacing** using the **Format → Line Spacing** option.

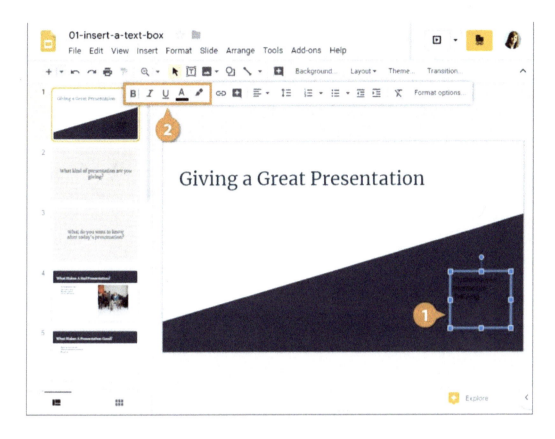

Adding Images & Videos

1. **Insert an Image**
   - Click **Insert → Image** and choose the source of the image (Upload from computer, Google Drive, or Search the web).

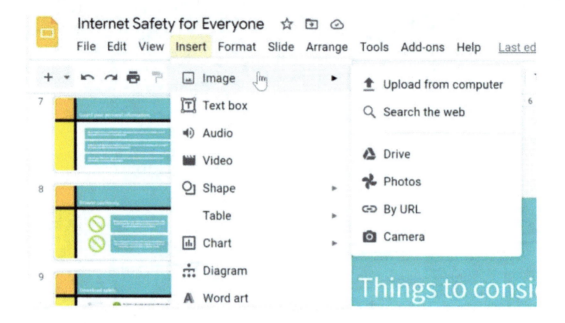

- ○ Once inserted, resize and position the image by dragging its corners.

2. **Adding a Video**
   - ○ Click **Insert → Video** and search for videos on YouTube or upload a video file from your computer or Google Drive.

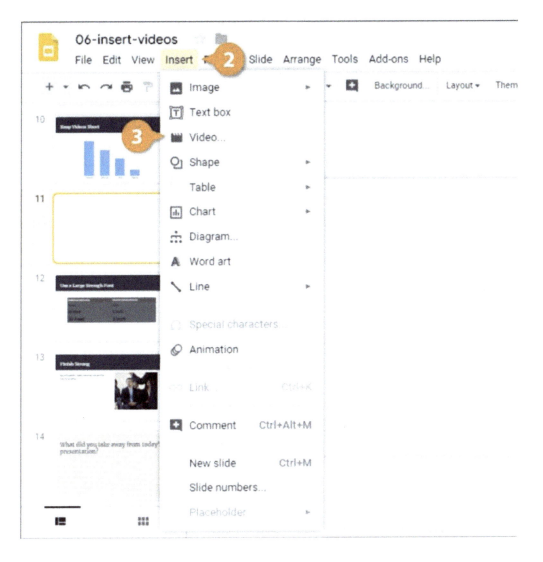

o Resize and position the video as needed.

3. **Using Image Editing Tools**
   o Right-click on any image to access the **Image Options** menu. You can adjust the **brightness, contrast**, or even **crop** the image.

💡 Tip: Use **Google Drawings** (Insert → Drawing) to create custom graphics and import them directly into your slides.

Applying Slide Transitions & Animations

Slide transitions and animations can help keep your audience engaged by adding movement and effects.

Slide Transitions

1. **Applying Transitions**
   - Select the slide you want to apply a transition to.
   - Click **Slide → Transition**.

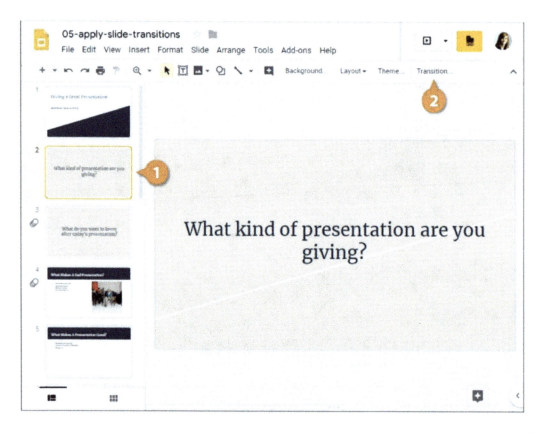

   - In the panel on the right, choose from various transitions like **Fade**, **Slide from Right**, or **Cube Rotate**.

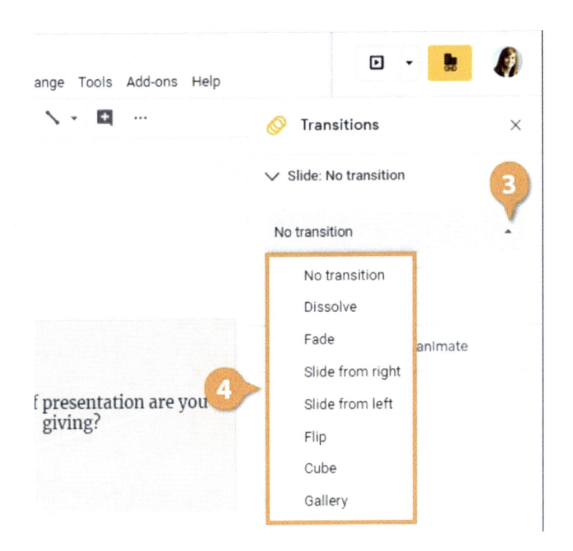

- Adjust the **speed** of the transition with the slider.

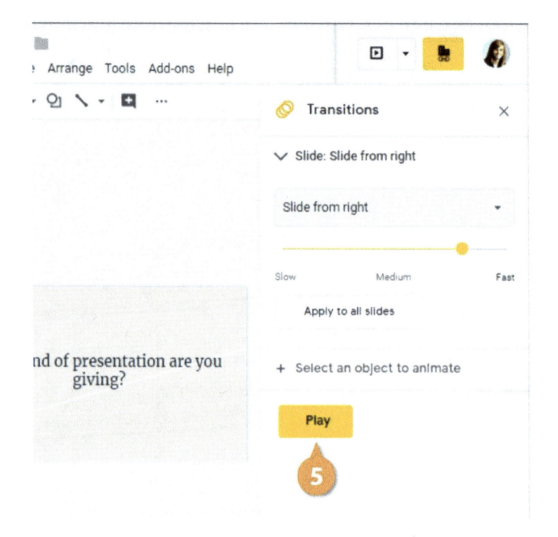

2. **Customizing Transitions**
   o You can apply the same transition to all slides by clicking **Apply to All Slides** at the bottom of the transitions panel.
   o **Preview** the transition by clicking the **Play** button.

Animating Objects

1. **Adding Animations**
   o Click on the object (text, image, shape, etc.) you want to animate.
   o Click **Insert → Animation**.

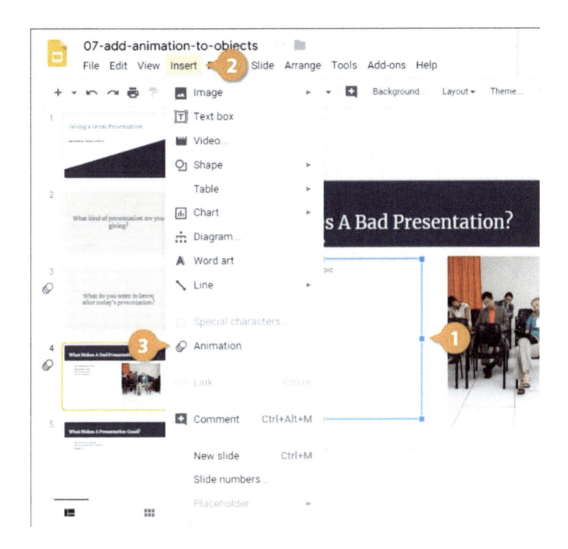

> ○ In the panel, choose the animation type, such as **Fade In**, **Zoom In**, or **Fly In**.

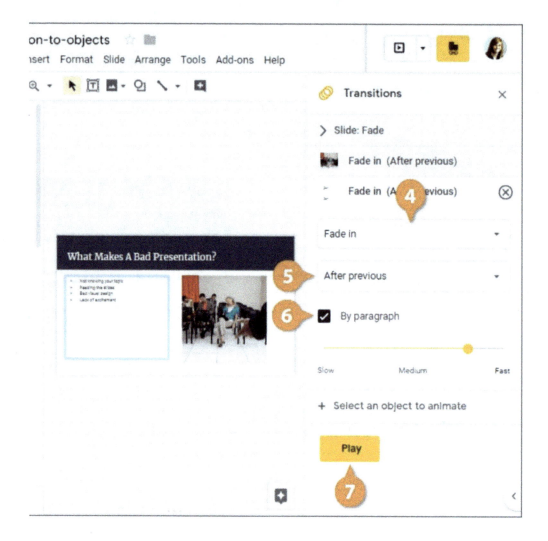

- o Adjust the **animation timing** (on-click, after previous, or with previous).
2. **Fine-Tuning Animations**
   - o Set the **speed** of the animation and add **delays** for a smoother flow.
   - o **Preview** animations by clicking the **Play** button in the animation panel.

💡 *Tip: Apply simple animations for a professional look. Too many animations can be distracting.*

Presenting with Speaker Notes

Google Slides has an excellent **Speaker Notes** feature that allows you to add notes for each slide to guide your presentation. These notes are visible only to you and not your audience.

Adding Speaker Notes

1. **Open Speaker Notes Section**
   - At the bottom of the slide, click the **Click to add speaker notes** area.
   - Type any additional notes you want to remember while presenting (e.g., key points or explanations).

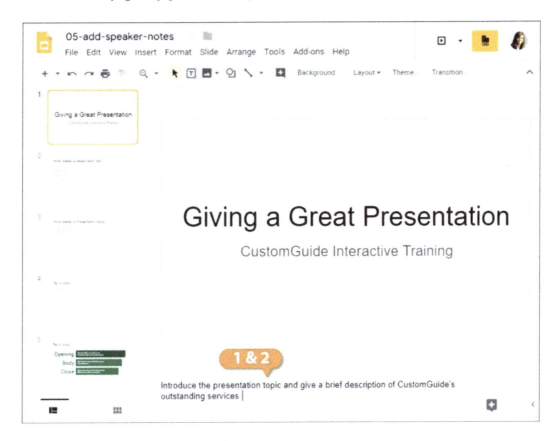

2. **Presenting with Notes**
    - ○ When you start the presentation by clicking **Present** (top-right corner), you will see your slides full-screen.
    - ○ If you want to view the notes while presenting, click **Presenter View** from the **Slideshow → Presenter View** option.
    - ○ This opens a separate window that shows your speaker notes along with a preview of upcoming slides.

💡 *Tip: Use **keyboard shortcuts** like **Arrow keys** to navigate slides quickly during the presentation.*

PART 4: Time & Task Management

Chapter 11: Google Calendar – Managing Appointments & Events

G oogle Calendar is a powerful, cloud-based calendar tool that helps you stay organized and on top of your schedule. It allows users to **create events**, **set reminders**, **sync with others**, and easily manage their **appointments** and **meetings**. Google Calendar is fully integrated with other Google Workspace tools, such as Gmail and Google Meet, making it an essential tool for both personal and professional scheduling.

Creating & Scheduling Events

Google Calendar makes it easy to **create events** and **schedule appointments**, helping you organize your time more effectively.

Step-by-Step Instructions for Creating an Event

1. **Open Google Calendar**
   - Go to **calendar.google.com** in your browser or open the **Google Calendar app** on your phone.
   - Make sure you are signed in to your Google account.
2. **Create an Event**
   - On the left side of the calendar, click the **Create** button or click anywhere on the calendar.

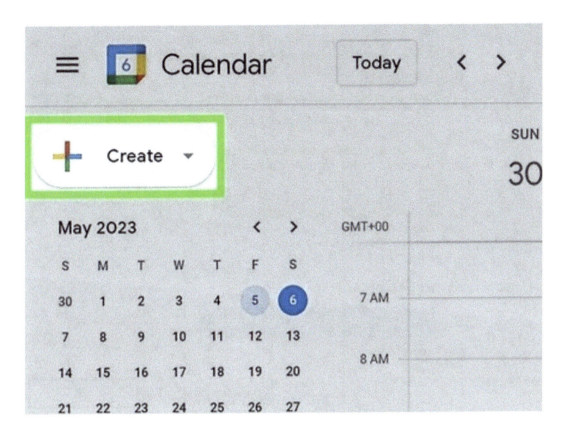

- ○ A pop-up window will appear where you can add event details such as the **title**, **date**, and **time**.

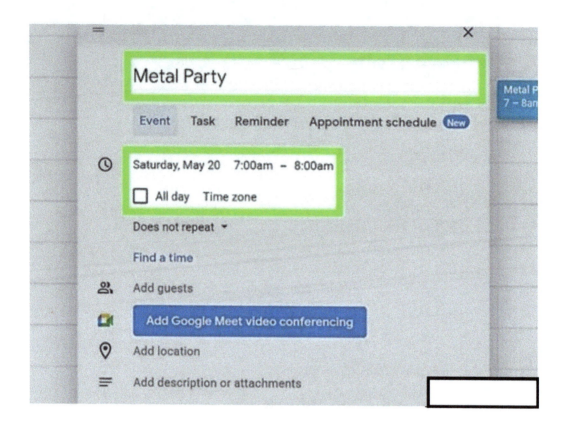

3. **Setting Event Details**
    - Enter the **Event Title**, such as "Meeting with Team" or "Doctor's Appointment".
    - Select the **Start date and time** and **End date and time**.
    - If your event is **recurring**, click on the **Does not repeat** drop-down to select the frequency (Daily, Weekly, Monthly, etc.).
4. **Event Location**
    - If the event has a physical location, add it in the **Location** field. You can also include a **Google Meet** link here, which will automatically be added if you're hosting an online meeting.
5. **Adding Guests**
    - Under the **Guests** section, enter the email addresses of people you want to invite to the event.
    - Google Calendar will send an invitation to your guests with the event details.

💡 *Tip: If you're scheduling a virtual meeting, add a **Google Meet** link by clicking on the **Add Google Meet video conferencing** button.*

Setting Up Reminders & Notifications

Staying on track is easier with **reminders** and **notifications**. Google Calendar allows you to customize how and when you're notified of upcoming events.

Step-by-Step Instructions for Setting Up Reminders

On Desktop (Web Browser)

1. **Open Google Calendar**
   - Go to Google Calendar and sign in to your Google account if you haven't already.
2. **Create a Reminder**
   - Click on the **"+ Create"** button in the top left corner.
   - Alternatively, click on the desired date and time directly on the calendar.
3. **Choose "Reminder"**
   - In the pop-up window, select **"Reminder"** instead of "Event."
4. **Enter Reminder Details**
   - Type the reminder text (e.g., "Call John at 3 PM").
   - Set the **date and time** for the reminder.
5. **Set Recurrence (Optional)**
   - If the reminder is recurring, click on **"Does not repeat"** and select an option (e.g., daily, weekly, custom).
6. **Save the Reminder**
   - Click **"Save"** to add the reminder to your calendar.

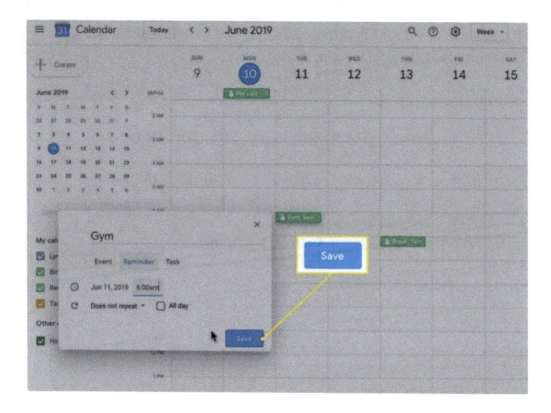

On Mobile (Android & iPhone)

1. **Open the Google Calendar App**
   - Download the Google Calendar app (Android) or <u>Google Calendar for iOS</u> if you don't have it.
2. **Tap the "+" Button**
   - Tap the **"+"** button (usually at the bottom-right corner).
3. **Select "Reminder"**
   - Choose **"Reminder"** from the options.
4. **Enter Reminder Details**
   - Type your reminder description.
   - Set the **date and time** for the reminder.
5. **Set Recurrence (If Needed)**
   - Tap **"Does not repeat"** to make it repeat daily, weekly, or on a custom schedule.
6. **Save the Reminder**
   - Tap **"Save"** to finalize your reminder.

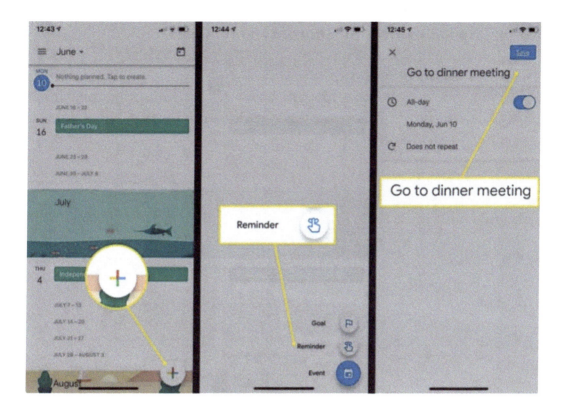

Managing and Deleting Reminders

- To **edit** a reminder, click or tap on it and modify the details.
- To **delete** a reminder, open it and click **"Delete"** or **trash icon**.

Once set, Google Calendar will notify you at the scheduled time. ⊙

💡 *Tip: Use **notifications** for events that require preparation, and **email reminders** for appointments you may need to prepare documents or information for.*

Sharing & Syncing Calendars with Others

Google Calendar makes it easy to share your calendar with colleagues, family, or friends, so everyone can stay updated on your schedule.

Step-by-Step Instructions for Sharing Your Calendar

1. **Go to Calendar Settings**
   - o On the left-hand sidebar, under **My calendars**, hover over the calendar you want to share, click on the **three vertical dots**, and select **Settings and sharing**.

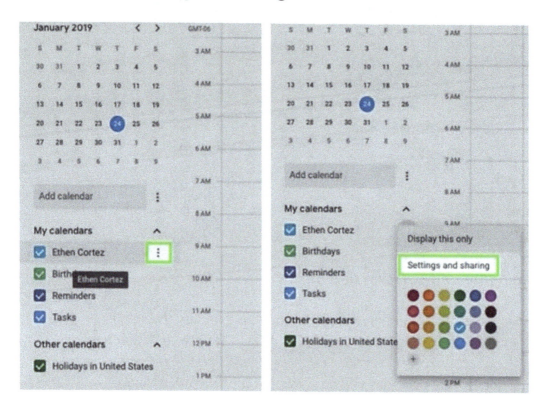

2. **Sharing with Individuals**
   - o In the **Share with specific people** section, click **Add people**.

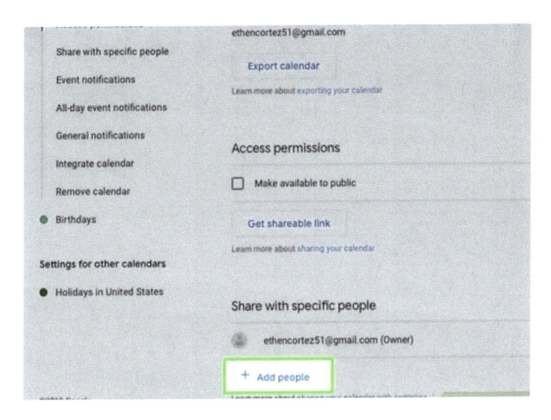

- o Enter the email addresses of the people you want to share your calendar with.
- o Choose their **permissions**
- o Click **Send** to send the invitation.

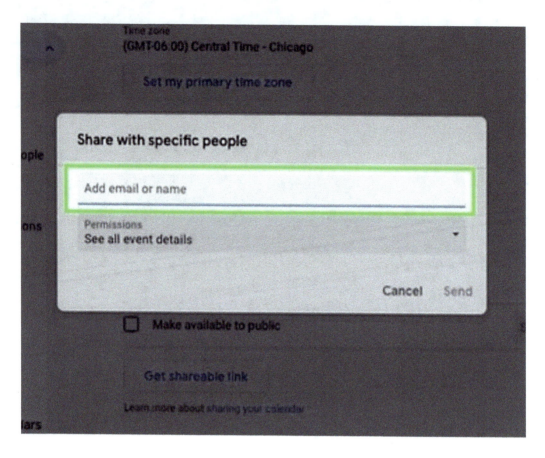

3. **Sharing with a Link**
   - If you want to share your calendar with anyone via a link, in the **Access permissions** section, select **Make available to public** or share a **view-only** link.

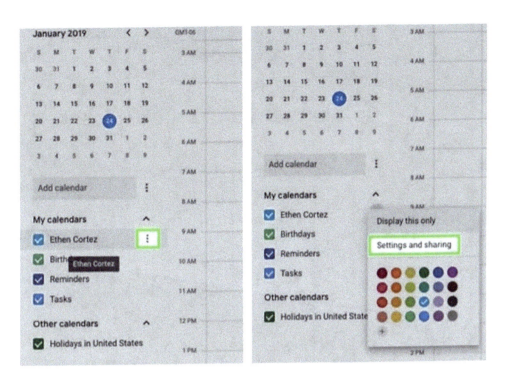

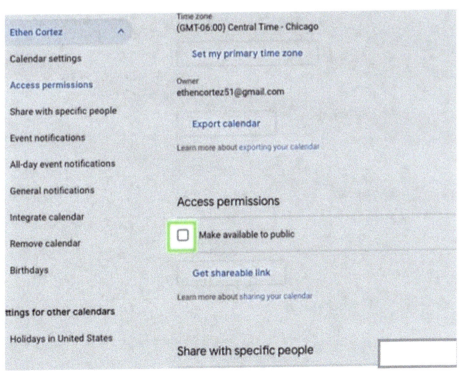

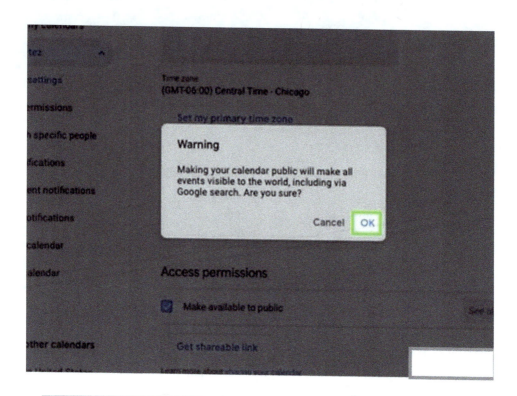

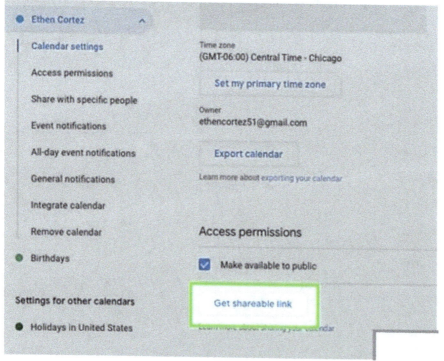

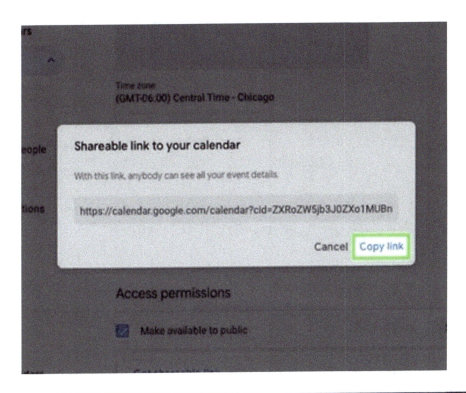

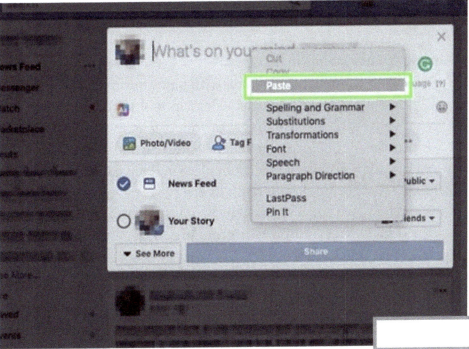

Paste and share your shareable link anywhere. You can share it in an email, on social media, or send it to a contact.

- This is useful for events or calendars that need to be publicly accessible.
4. **Syncing Calendars**
   - If you use multiple calendars (e.g., personal, work), you can sync them all in **Google Calendar** for easy viewing.
   - To view different calendars side by side, check or uncheck the boxes next to the calendar names on the left sidebar.

💡 *Tip: You can add calendars from other services (like Outlook or Apple) to Google Calendar by using the **Import** option in the calendar settings.*

Using Google Calendar with Gmail & Google Meet

Google Calendar integrates seamlessly with both **Gmail** and **Google Meet**, making it a central hub for all your scheduling needs.

Step-by-Step Instructions for Integrating Gmail & Google Meet

1. **Adding Events from Gmail**
   - When you receive an email with an event invitation (e.g., meeting or appointment), Google Calendar will automatically detect the event and suggest adding it to your calendar.
   - In Gmail, open the email, click **Add to Calendar**, and the event details will automatically populate in Google Calendar.
2. **Adding a Google Meet Link to an Event**
   - When creating a new event or editing an existing one, click **Add Google Meet video conferencing** to generate a unique **Google Meet link** for the event.
   - You can share this link with your guests to allow them to join the meeting virtually.
3. **Joining a Google Meet from Calendar**
   - On the day of your meeting, simply click the **Join with Google Meet** link from your calendar event to join the video call directly.

o This is especially useful when hosting virtual meetings, as all participants can access the link with a click.

💡 *Tip: You can automatically add a **Google Meet link** to all your events by enabling the feature in Google Calendar settings. This way, every event you create will have a virtual meeting link by default.*

Chapter 12: Google Keep – Organizing Notes & Ideas

Google Keep is a note-taking and organization tool that helps you quickly capture and organize ideas, reminders, and to-do lists. Whether you're working on a project or just need a place to jot down thoughts, Google Keep makes it easy to keep track of your notes. It syncs seamlessly across devices and integrates with other Google Workspace tools, making it a versatile tool for personal and professional use.

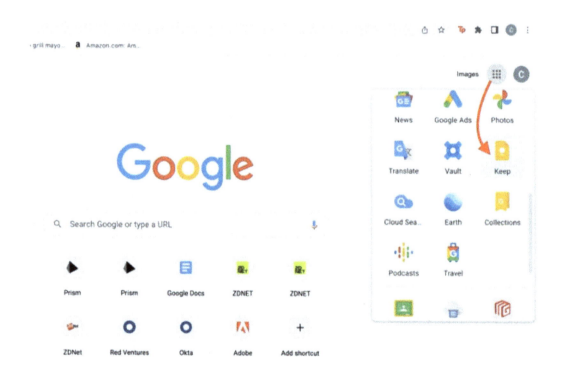

How to find Google Keep in your G Suite.

Creating & Formatting Notes

Google Keep allows you to quickly create notes and format them in various ways to make sure they suit your needs, whether you're making a to-do list, writing a reminder, or capturing an idea.

Step-by-Step Instructions for Creating a Note

1. **Opening Google Keep**
   - To begin, visit **keep.google.com** in your browser or open the **Google Keep** app on your mobile device.
   - Make sure you're signed in to your Google account to ensure your notes sync across devices.
2. **Creating a New Note**
   - On the main screen, click the **Take a note** section at the top.

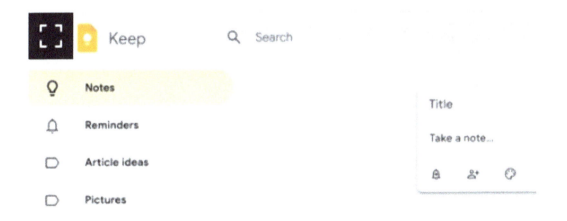

   - You can start typing your note right away. If you're using the app, tap the **Plus** icon to begin a new note.
3. **Formatting Your Note**
   - Once your note is created, you can format the text by clicking the **three vertical dots** for more options.

- You can **bold**, **italicize**, or **underline** text, as well as use bullet points and numbered lists.

4. **Adding a Title**
   - To make your note more organized, you can add a **title** to it. Simply type in the title field at the top before writing the body of your note.

💡 *Tip: For longer notes, break them into smaller sections by using bullet points or headers to make them easier to read.*

Using Labels & Color Codes for Organization

To stay organized, Google Keep offers several ways to **categorize** and **color-code** your notes. This helps you easily locate notes by theme, urgency, or project.

Step-by-Step Instructions for Using Labels & Color Codes

1. **Adding Labels**
   - After creating a note, click on the **three vertical dots** at the top of the note and select **Add label**.

- o You can create new labels or select existing ones. For example, you could create labels like **Work**, **Personal**, or **Ideas** to organize your notes by category.
- o Once labels are applied, you can easily view all notes with the same label by clicking on the **Label** in the left sidebar.

2. **Using Color Codes**
   - o To give each note a distinct visual identity, Google Keep allows you to **assign colors** to your notes.
   - o After creating a note, click on the **Palette icon** at the bottom of the note and choose a color.
   - o Color coding can help you visually categorize your notes, so you can find them quickly by color association.

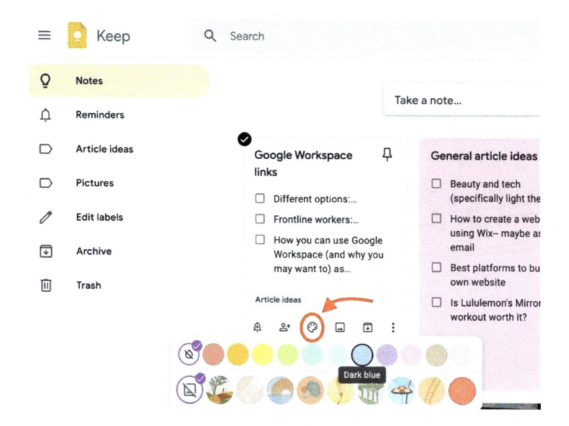

💡 *Tip: Use colors for different priority levels, e.g., red for urgent, green for completed tasks, blue for personal, etc. This visual system will help you manage your notes more efficiently.*

Setting Reminders & Syncing Across Devices

Google Keep allows you to **set reminders** for your notes, ensuring that you never forget important tasks. Reminders sync across all devices, so you will receive notifications wherever you are.

Step-by-Step Instructions for Setting Reminders

1. **Adding a Reminder**
   - Open the note you want to set a reminder for.

○ At the bottom of the note, click the **Remind me** button (bell icon).

○ Choose to set a **time-based reminder** (e.g., a reminder at a specific time or day) or a **location-based reminder** (e.g., remind me when I arrive at a specific place).

○ If using the mobile app, tap the **Reminder** icon and select the time or location.

2. **Setting Recurring Reminders**

○ For tasks that repeat, you can set recurring reminders in Google Keep.

○ To do this, after selecting a reminder time, click on the **Repeat** option to choose how often the reminder should repeat (daily, weekly, monthly, etc.).

3. **Syncing Notes Across Devices**

○ Google Keep automatically **syncs** all of your notes and reminders across devices, as long as you're signed in to the same Google account.

○ Whether you use your phone, tablet, or computer, any change made to a note will be reflected in real-time across all devices.

💡 *Tip: Enable **notifications** for reminders so that you never miss an important task. You can adjust these settings in your phone's notification center or through the Google Keep settings.*

Chapter 13: Google Tasks – Managing To-Do Lists

G oogle Tasks is a simple yet powerful tool designed to help you stay organized and manage your to-do lists effectively. Integrated with other Google Workspace apps like Gmail and Google Calendar, it provides an efficient way to create, track, and manage tasks and deadlines, keeping you on top of your responsibilities whether at work or in your personal life.

Creating Tasks & Subtasks

Google Tasks allows you to create a variety of tasks and break them down into subtasks for better organization. Whether you're managing a project, a shopping list, or just your daily to-dos, Google Tasks makes it easy to capture tasks and keep track of them.

Step-by-Step Instructions for Creating Tasks

1. **Opening Google Tasks**
   - Access Google Tasks by clicking on the **Tasks** icon, usually located on the right side of your Gmail or Google Calendar page.

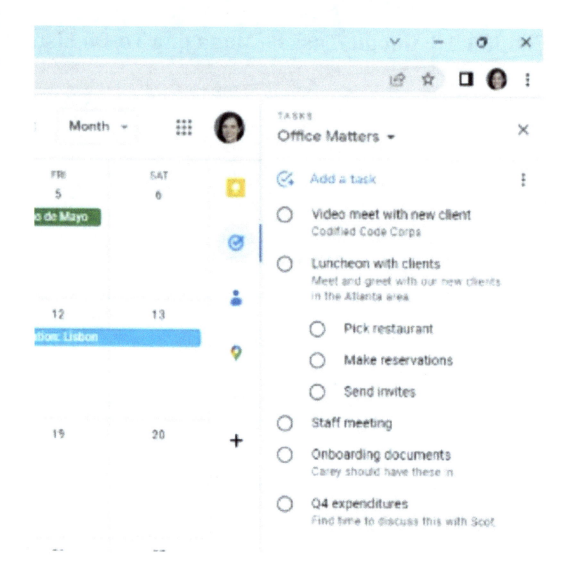

- You can also use the Google Tasks app on your mobile device for on-the-go task management.

2. **Creating a New Task**
   - On the Google Tasks panel, click the **Add a task** button or type in the field that says "Add a task."
   - Enter a title for your task in the provided space. This should be brief yet descriptive (e.g., "Finish project report" or "Pick up groceries").
   - Press **Enter** or **Return** to save your task.

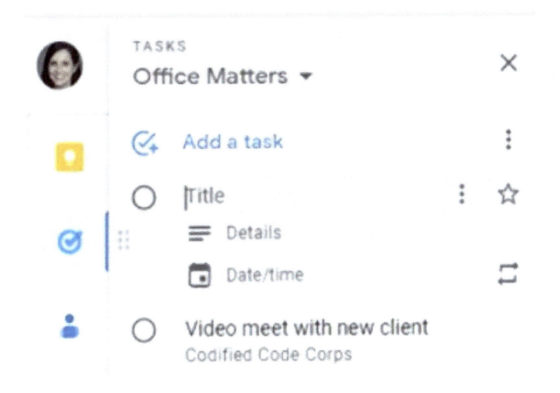

TASKS

Office Matters ▾

Add a task

◯ Title

≡ Details

📅 Date/time

◯ Video meet with new client
Codified Code Corps

3. **Adding Details to a Task**
   - Click on a task to open it, and you can add more details such as **due dates** and **subtasks**.
   - For example, if your task is "Prepare presentation," you can open it up and add subtasks like "Design slides," "Write script," and "Rehearse."

Step-by-Step Instructions for Creating Subtasks

1. **Adding Subtasks to Tasks**
   - After creating a task, click on it to open it in more detail.
   - You will see an option labeled **Add a subtask**. Click on it.

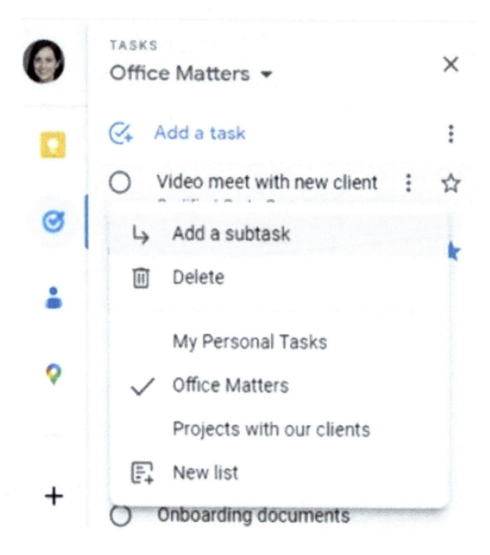

- Enter the subtask title (e.g., "Write introduction") and press **Enter**.
- Repeat this for each subtask you want to add. Subtasks can be checked off as they are completed, helping you stay organized and on track.

💡 *Tip: Breaking large tasks into smaller, manageable subtasks makes it easier to focus and stay productive.*

Integrating Tasks with Gmail & Google Calendar

Google Tasks integrates seamlessly with Gmail and Google Calendar, which helps to keep all your tasks synchronized with your email and calendar schedule.

Step-by-Step Instructions for Integrating with Gmail

1. **Creating Tasks from Gmail**
   - When reading an email in Gmail, you can quickly turn it into a task by clicking on the **More Options** button (three dots) at the top-right of the email.
   - Select **Add to Tasks**. This will automatically create a task with the email subject as the task title.
   - You can click on the task and add more details or set due dates if needed.
2. **Viewing Tasks in Gmail**
   - Once tasks are added, they will appear in the Google Tasks sidebar, allowing you to easily reference and manage them while working in Gmail.
   - Tasks in Gmail are automatically synced with your Google Tasks app, making it easy to manage everything in one place.

Step-by-Step Instructions for Integrating with Google Calendar

1. **Viewing Tasks in Google Calendar**
   - Any task you add a **due date** to will automatically appear in **Google Calendar** as an all-day event.
   - Open Google Calendar and check the **Tasks** calendar in the left sidebar to view your due tasks.
2. **Creating Calendar Events from Tasks**
   - If you need to add a task to your calendar as a time-specific event, simply click on a task with a due date.
   - From the task detail view, you can adjust the task to show up at a specific time in Google Calendar by adding a **time slot**.

🔹 Tip: Integrating Google Tasks with Gmail and Calendar ensures you don't miss any deadlines or action items from your emails, keeping you organized and on top of your responsibilities.

Setting Deadlines & Reminders

Google Tasks allows you to set due dates and reminders for tasks, helping you stay on track and be more productive.

Step-by-Step Instructions for Setting Deadlines

1. **Setting a Due Date**
   - Click on any task to open it.
   - Next to the task title, you'll see an option for **Add due date**. Click on this to select a calendar date when the task is due.
   - Once set, the task will appear in your Google Calendar as a due event.
2. **Setting Reminders for Tasks**
   - If you want to receive a reminder before a task's due date, click on the task to open it and look for **Add reminder**.
   - Choose the time when you'd like to be reminded (e.g., 1 day before, 1 hour before, etc.), and you'll receive a notification in your Google Calendar or mobile device.

Managing and Completing Tasks

1. **Marking Tasks as Complete**
   - When you've completed a task or subtask, simply click the checkbox next to it to mark it as done. It will be removed from your active task list but will still appear in your **completed tasks**.
   - You can also delete completed tasks by clicking on the task and selecting **Delete** from the options.
2. **Editing Tasks**

o   If you need to adjust a task's details (such as the title, due date, or reminder), click on the task to edit the information and save the changes.

💡 *Tip: Set **reminders** for your most important tasks to ensure they're not forgotten and stay at the top of your priority list.*

PART 5: Business & Team Tools

Chapter 14: Google Sites – Creating Websites Without Coding

Google Sites is a user-friendly website-building tool that allows anyone to create a professional-looking website without needing to know how to code. Whether you're making a portfolio, a project website, or a site for your business, Google Sites provides all the tools you need to get started quickly.

Creating a Website Using Google Sites

Google Sites is a simple, drag-and-drop platform for creating websites. You don't need any technical expertise to get started. You can create, design, and publish a website all from within your Google Workspace account.

Step-by-Step Instructions for Creating a Website

1. **Accessing Google Sites**
   - To begin creating a website, open **Google Sites** by navigating to **sites.google.com** or access it via the Google Apps menu on your Google Workspace homepage.
   - If you're using Google Workspace, sign in with your credentials, and you'll be taken to your dashboard.
2. **Starting a New Site**
   - Click the **+** button to create a new website.
   - You'll be given the option to start with a **blank template** or choose from pre-made **templates** like "Portfolio" or "Project."
   - Select a template or choose the blank template to create a site from scratch.

3. **Choosing a Site Name**
   ○ Once you start a new site, enter a **site name** at the top of the page. This name will also be the main title of your website.
   ○ You can change this at any time by clicking on the title area.

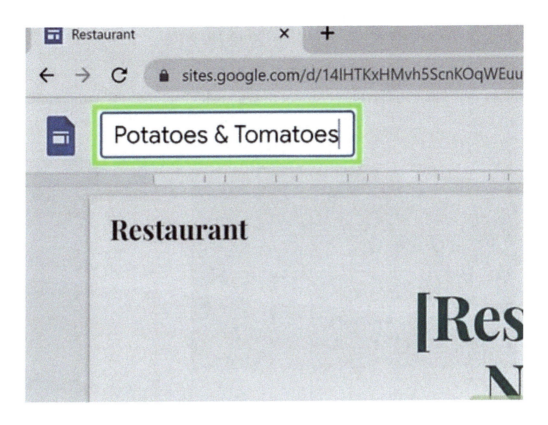

4. **Adding Content**
    - Google Sites works on a simple **drag-and-drop** interface. You can add text, images, videos, and other elements to your page by clicking on the content options on the right-hand sidebar.
    - Simply drag the desired element (like text box or image) to your page layout.

💡 *Tip: Keep your website clean and professional by sticking to a simple design layout that highlights your key content. Avoid overcrowding the page with unnecessary elements.*

Customizing Layouts & Adding Pages

Once your site is created, you'll want to customize the layout and add pages to organize your content.

Step-by-Step Instructions for Customizing Layouts

1. **Choosing a Layout**
   - Click on the **Insert** tab in the right sidebar, and you'll find multiple options for layouts (e.g., **two-column layouts**, **image layouts**).

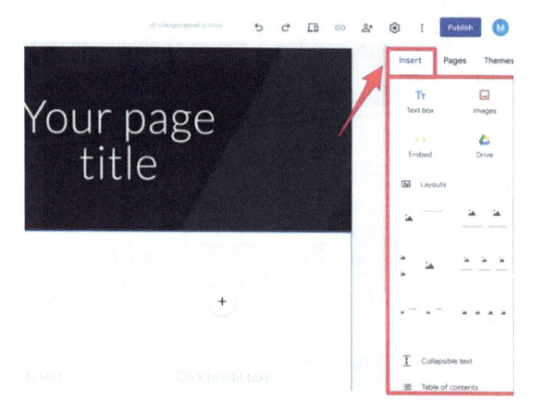

   - Select the layout style you prefer and drag it to your page.
   - Once you drop the layout, you can begin adding content to each section of the layout.
2. **Editing Layouts**
   - You can always change a layout by selecting a section and clicking on the pencil icon to edit it.
   - Adjust text size, font, and color through the formatting options at the top.
3. **Adding Images & Videos**

o To add images, click on the **Images** tab in the sidebar. You can upload images from your computer or use images from Google Drive or search the web directly through the platform.

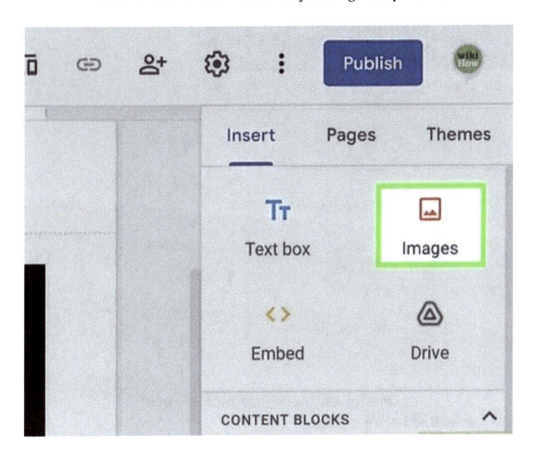

o For videos, select the **YouTube** tab if you want to embed a video, or upload it from your Google Drive.

Step-by-Step Instructions for Adding Pages

1. **Adding New Pages to Your Site**
   o To add a page, click the **Pages** tab in the right-hand sidebar.
   o Click the **+** icon at the bottom of the sidebar, and enter the page name (e.g., "About Us" or "Contact").

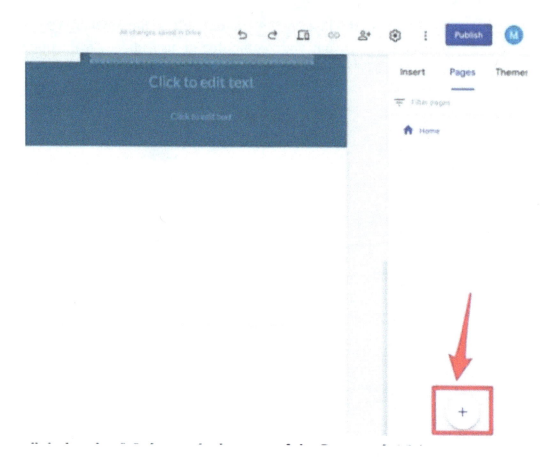

- Select **Done** to add the page to your website.
2. **Navigating Between Pages**
    - You can easily switch between pages using the navigation bar at the top of your site.
    - As you add more pages, Google Sites automatically updates the navigation bar so visitors can move through your site.
3. **Organizing Pages**
    - You can rearrange pages in the sidebar to change their order or create **subpages** by dragging a page under another.
    - Organize your pages logically so that visitors can easily find what they're looking for.

💡 Tip: When adding pages, think about the user experience. Keep navigation simple, and use clear, descriptive titles for your pages.

Publishing & Managing Permissions

After you've customized and added all your content, you can publish your site and control who has access to it.

Step-by-Step Instructions for Publishing Your Site

1. **Previewing Your Site**
   - Before publishing, click on the **Preview** button to see how your site will look to visitors.
   - Make any adjustments to the layout, images, or content based on the preview.

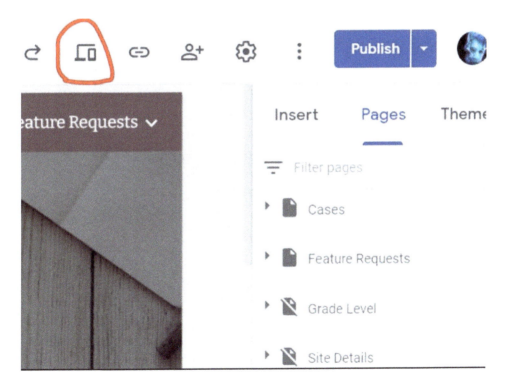

2. **Publishing the Site**
   - Once you're satisfied with your site, click on the **Publish** button in the top-right corner.

- ○ Google Sites will ask you to choose a unique web address for your site (e.g., **sites.google.com/view/yoursite**).
- ○ After selecting your address, click **Publish** again.

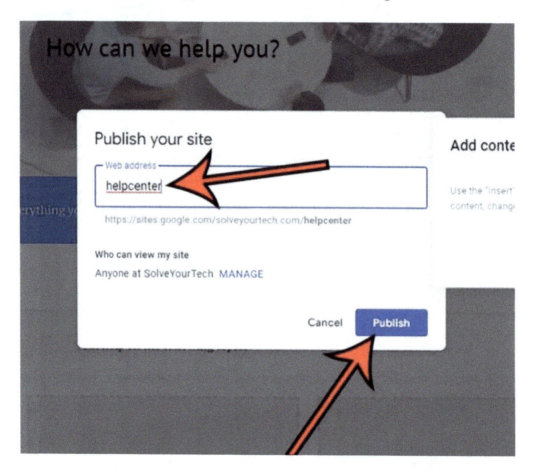

3. **Managing Site Settings**
   - ○ You can edit site settings such as **site name**, **theme**, or **access settings** at any time by clicking the **gear icon** in the upper-right corner.
   - ○ Google Sites automatically saves your changes, so you can go back and update your site without needing to republish every time.

Step-by-Step Instructions for Managing Permissions

1. **Setting Permissions for Who Can View or Edit Your Site**

- To manage access, click the **Share with others** button in the top-right corner of the screen.

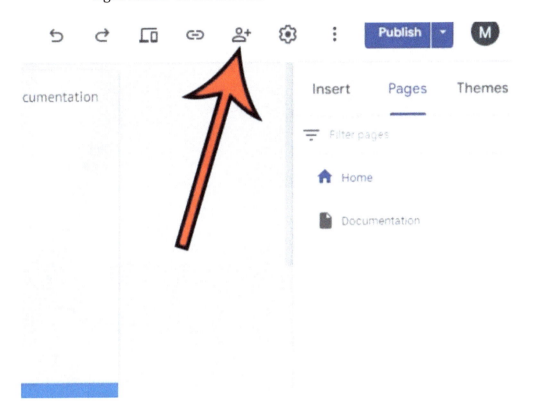

- You'll be prompted to add individuals or groups and assign them specific roles: **Viewer**, **Editor**, or **Owner**.

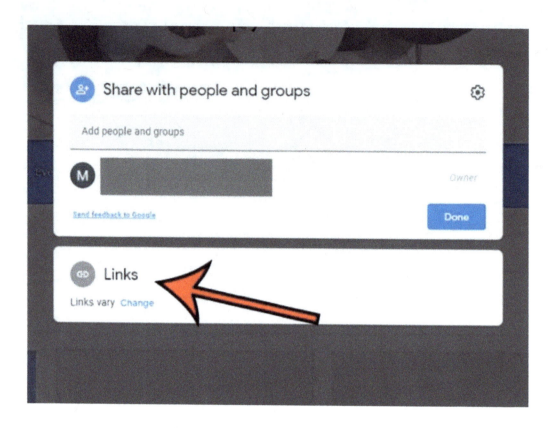

- You can also select **Anyone with the link** or limit access to specific people within your organization.

2. **Changing Site Permissions**
   - If you need to change permissions, return to the **Share** settings and adjust the visibility or roles for specific users.

💡 *Tip: Be mindful of your site's permissions. If you're sharing the site with a wider audience, consider making it public or sharing a link. For sensitive content, restrict access to specific individuals or groups.*

Chapter 15: Google Admin Console – Managing Google Workspace for Business

The **Google Admin Console** is the control center for managing your organization's Google Workspace services. It provides administrators with a centralized platform to oversee user accounts, settings, permissions, security, and other important functions. This chapter will guide you through the process of adding and managing users, assigning roles and permissions, and monitoring security and compliance within the Admin Console.

Adding & Managing Users

In Google Workspace, users represent the employees, contractors, or collaborators in your organization. The Admin Console allows you to easily add, manage, and delete users as your organization evolves. As an administrator, you can control access to services, assign specific roles, and configure settings tailored to each user.

Step-by-Step Instructions for Adding a User

1. **Access the Google Admin Console**
   o First, sign in to your **Google Admin Console** at **admin.google.com** using your administrator credentials.
   o Once logged in, you'll be taken to the Admin Console dashboard where you can manage all aspects of your Google Workspace account.
2. **Adding a New User**
   o From the Admin Console, click on the **Users** section. This will show a list of all the users in your organization.

- To add a new user, click on the **Add New User** button.

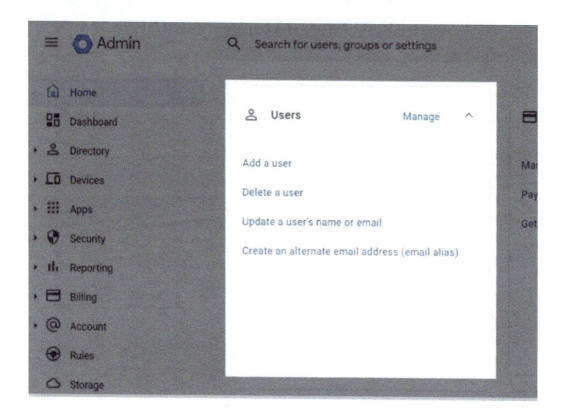

- A form will appear asking for the new user's details. Fill in the required fields, including:
  - **Full Name**
  - **Email Address**
  - **Password** (you can either set a temporary password or let the user create their own).
- Once all details are filled in, click **Add New User**. The user will receive a notification with their account information, including a link to set their password.

3. **Managing User Information**
   - After adding a user, you can edit their details by clicking on their profile in the Admin Console.

- You can change the user's **name**, **email address**, **password**, and assign them to specific **organizational units** within your company (e.g., departments or teams).
- You can also configure their access to certain Google Workspace tools, such as Gmail, Google Drive, and Google Meet.

Step-by-Step Instructions for Deleting a User

1. **Select the User**: In the **Users** section, click on the user's name you wish to delete.
2. **Delete the User**: Click on the **More** button (three vertical dots) at the top-right corner of the user's profile page and select **Delete User**.
3. **Confirm Deletion**: You will be prompted to confirm the deletion of the user. When a user is deleted, their data will be removed from Google Workspace, but you will have an option to transfer their data to another user before deletion.

💡 *Tip: Always back up important data before deleting a user account to avoid any loss of critical information.*

Assigning Roles & Permissions

In Google Workspace, roles and permissions define what each user can access and manage within the system. Assigning appropriate roles ensures that users have the tools and permissions they need to perform their job without compromising security or privacy.

Step-by-Step Instructions for Assigning Roles

1. **Navigate to User Profile**
   - From the **Users** section in the Admin Console, select the user for whom you want to assign a role.
2. **Assigning a Role**

- Within the user's profile page, click on the **Roles and Privileges** tab.
- Click the **Assign Role** button. You will be presented with a list of predefined roles available in your organization (such as **Super Admin**, **Groups Admin**, **User Management Admin**, etc.).
- Select the appropriate role based on the user's responsibilities. For example:
  - **Super Admin**: Full access to all Admin Console features.
  - **Groups Admin**: Manage user groups and distribution lists.
  - **Help Desk Admin**: Manage user accounts and provide basic support.
  - **Billing Admin**: Manage billing and subscription settings.

3. **Custom Roles (Optional)**
  - You can also create **custom roles** tailored to your organization's needs. To do this:
    - Navigate to the **Admin roles** section.
    - Click **Create Role** and name the role.
    - Customize permissions based on the tools and services the role should have access to (e.g., Gmail, Calendar, Drive, etc.).
    - After creating the custom role, return to the user's profile to assign it.

💡 *Tip: Regularly review user roles to ensure that users have the appropriate access level, especially after role changes or organizational shifts.*

Monitoring Security & Compliance

Security and compliance are critical components of managing Google Workspace for business. The Admin Console provides various tools for monitoring the security status of your organization's accounts, reviewing security reports, and ensuring compliance with internal policies and industry regulations.

Step-by-Step Instructions for Monitoring Security

1. **Accessing Security Settings**
   - From the Admin Console dashboard, click on the **Security** section to access your organization's security settings.
   - Here, you can configure various security policies such as **password strength**, **two-factor authentication (2FA)** enforcement, and **data encryption**.
2. **Viewing Security Reports**
   - Click on the **Security Reports** tab to view detailed reports on activities such as user logins, failed login attempts, and other security-related events.
   - You can filter reports by user, time frame, and event type to focus on specific security concerns.
3. **Configuring Alerts**
   - Within the Security section, you can set up **alerts** to notify you of suspicious activities or changes in your Google Workspace environment.
   - Examples of useful alerts include:
     - **Multiple failed login attempts**
     - **Account sign-ins from unfamiliar locations**
     - **Changes to user roles or permissions**
4. **Compliance Monitoring**
   - Use the **Reports** section to monitor and track compliance with your organization's internal policies and any industry-specific regulations.
   - Google Workspace offers a **Compliance Center** where you can manage settings for things like **data retention**, **email archiving**, and **audit logs**.
5. **User Activity Logs**
   - Review activity logs to track user actions within Google Workspace, such as file sharing, document edits, and account changes.
   - You can filter the logs by user, event type, or time to gain insight into user behavior and ensure compliance with company policies.

💡 *Tip: Set up automatic security audits to monitor potential security threats regularly. Proactive monitoring helps catch issues before they escalate into larger security breaches.*

PART 6: Automation & Advanced Features

Chapter 16: Google Apps Script – Automating Google Workspace

Google Apps Script is a powerful tool that allows you to extend and automate the functionality of various Google Workspace applications, such as Google Docs, Sheets, Gmail, and Google Drive. By writing scripts in JavaScript, you can automate tasks, customize workflows, and create add-ons for Google Workspace tools. This chapter will introduce you to the basics of Google Apps Script and show you how to write simple scripts and create custom add-ons.

Introduction to Google Apps Script

Google Apps Script is a cloud-based scripting language developed by Google. It is built on JavaScript and enables you to automate repetitive tasks, integrate Google Workspace applications, and add custom functionality without needing to install any software or worry about servers.

Google Apps Script is tightly integrated with Google Workspace tools, allowing you to work directly with documents, spreadsheets, calendars, emails, and more. With just a few lines of code, you can automate almost any aspect of Google Workspace, such as sending personalized emails, managing data in spreadsheets, or creating custom document templates.

Key Features of Google Apps Script:

- **Automation**: Automate repetitive tasks like sending reports, updating data, or syncing calendars.
- **Custom Functions**: Create custom functions in Sheets and Docs that are tailored to your needs.

- **Triggers**: Set up triggers to run scripts at specific times or when certain events occur (e.g., when a form is submitted).
- **Web Apps**: Build and deploy web apps that integrate with your Google Workspace environment.
- **Add-ons**: Create custom add-ons for Google Docs, Sheets, and other Google Workspace tools.

Writing Basic Scripts to Automate Tasks

Google Apps Script can help you automate simple tasks like sending emails, organizing files, or creating events in your calendar. Below is a step-by-step guide to creating a basic script that sends automated emails.

Step-by-Step Instructions for Writing a Basic Script

1. **Access Google Apps Script**
   - Open any Google Workspace tool, such as **Google Sheets** or **Google Docs**.
   - Click on **Extensions** in the menu, then select **Apps Script**. This will open the Google Apps Script editor where you can write and run your code.

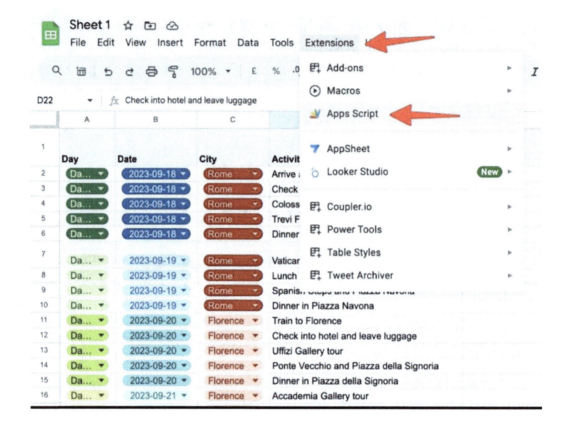

2. **Write Your Script**
   - In the script editor, you'll see a blank space where you can write your script.
   - For example, to send an email using Google Apps Script, enter the following code:

```
function sendEmail() {
  var recipient = 'example@example.com';
  var subject = 'Automated Email';
  var body = 'Hello, this is an automated email sent by Google Apps Script!';
  MailApp.sendEmail(recipient, subject, body);
}
```

1. This simple script sends an email to the specified recipient with the given subject and body.

2. **Save & Run the Script**
   - ○ Click **File** > **Save** to save your script. You can name your project if desired.
   - ○ To run the script, click the **Run** button (the triangle icon). The script will execute, and the email will be sent automatically.

3. **Set Permissions**
   - ○ The first time you run the script, Google will prompt you to authorize the script to access your Google services (e.g., Gmail). Click **Review Permissions**, choose your Google account, and click **Allow** to grant permission.

💡 *Tip: For more complex automation, you can create scripts that run on a schedule or in response to triggers, such as when a new row is added to a Google Sheet or when a form is submitted.*

Creating Custom Google Docs & Sheets Add-ons

Google Apps Script also allows you to build custom add-ons for Google Docs and Sheets. These add-ons can extend the functionality of your documents and spreadsheets, making them more efficient and tailored to your needs.

Step-by-Step Instructions for Creating a Custom Google Sheets Add-on

1. **Open Google Sheets and Access Apps Script**
   - ○ Open a Google Sheet where you want to add the functionality.
   - ○ Go to **Extensions** > **Apps Script** to open the script editor.

2. **Write the Add-on Script**
   - ○ In the script editor, write a script that will add functionality to your Google Sheets document. For example, the following script will create a custom menu in your Google Sheet to calculate the sum of selected cells:

```
function onOpen() {
  var ui = SpreadsheetApp.getUi();
  ui.createMenu('Custom Menu')
    .addItem('Sum Selected Cells', 'sumSelectedCells')
    .addToUi();
}


function sumSelectedCells() {
  var range = SpreadsheetApp.getActiveSpreadsheet().getActiveRange();
  var values = range.getValues();
  var sum = 0;
  for (var i = 0; i < values.length; i++) {
    for (var j = 0; j < values[i].length; j++) {
      sum += values[i][j];
    }
  }
  SpreadsheetApp.getUi().alert('The sum is: ' + sum);
}
```

1. This script creates a new menu in the Google Sheets interface and adds a custom item to calculate the sum of selected cells.
2. **Save & Deploy the Add-on**
   - After writing your script, save your project by clicking **File** > **Save**.
   - You can now use your custom add-on by refreshing the Google Sheet. The custom menu should appear, allowing you to run the function you created (e.g., calculating the sum of selected cells).
3. **Publish the Add-on**
   - To share the add-on with others or make it publicly available, you can deploy it by selecting **Publish** > **Deploy as add-on**. You will need to follow the prompts to submit your add-on for approval if you want it available to all users.

💡 *Tip: When creating add-ons, be mindful of the permissions your script needs. For example, an add-on that accesses user data (e.g., reading emails) will require explicit permissions.*

Chapter 17: Google Workspace Integrations & Third-Party Apps

Google Workspace is a versatile suite of tools that can be enhanced even further with integrations and third-party apps. These integrations allow you to connect Google Workspace with other applications you use daily, automate workflows, and boost productivity. Whether you're connecting Google Workspace with project management tools like Trello and Asana or automating processes through Zapier, these integrations can significantly improve your work efficiency.

In this chapter, we will explore how to integrate Google Workspace with other tools, automate tasks using **Zapier**, connect with popular project management tools like **Slack**, **Trello**, and **Asana**, and improve your workflow with **Chrome extensions**.

Connecting Google Workspace with Zapier

Zapier is a popular automation tool that allows you to connect Google Workspace with thousands of other apps. With Zapier, you can set up automated workflows called **Zaps** that trigger actions in one app based on events in another. This integration can save time and reduce manual work by automating repetitive tasks.

Step-by-Step Guide to Connecting Google Workspace with Zapier

1. **Sign Up for Zapier**
   - Go to zapier.com and sign up for a free account.
   - After signing in, you'll be directed to the Zapier dashboard, where you can create your first workflow (Zap).

2. **Create a New Zap**
    o Click **Create Zap** to start building your automation.

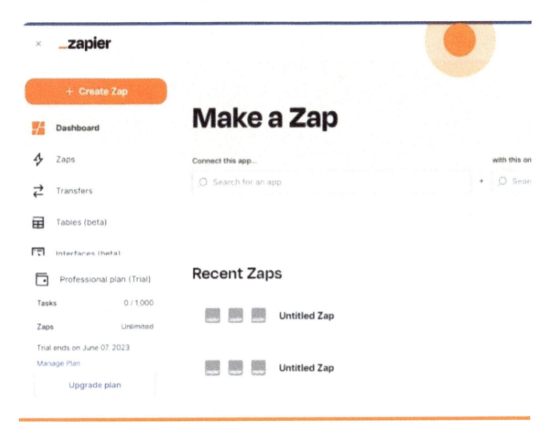

    o Zapier will prompt you to choose a **Trigger App**. For example, select **Google Sheets** to trigger an action when a new row is added to your sheet.
3. **Choose the Trigger Event**
    o After selecting Google Sheets, choose the trigger event. In this case, select **New Spreadsheet Row**.

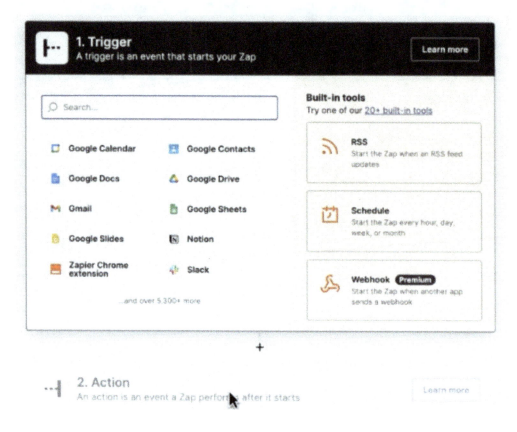

     o   You'll be asked to link your Google Sheets account to Zapier. Grant the necessary permissions for Zapier to access your Google Sheets data.

4. **Set Up the Action App**
   - o Next, choose the **Action App**. For example, select **Slack** if you want to send a message to a Slack channel when a new row is added to Google Sheets.
   - o You will need to sign in to your Slack account and choose the channel where you want the message to be sent.

5. **Test the Zap**
   - o After setting up the trigger and action, test the Zap to ensure it works as expected.
   - o If everything looks good, you can turn on your Zap, and it will run automatically whenever the trigger event occurs.

Tip: Zapier has a free plan with limited tasks per month. However, you can upgrade to a paid plan if you need more tasks or advanced features.

Using Google Workspace with Slack, Trello & Asana

Slack, **Trello**, and **Asana** are popular third-party apps used for team communication, task management, and collaboration. Integrating these apps with Google Workspace can help centralize your workflows, improve collaboration, and streamline project management.

Integrating Google Workspace with Slack

1. **Add the Google Workspace App to Slack**
   - Open Slack and navigate to the **Apps** section in the sidebar.
   - Search for the **Google Workspace** app (formerly G Suite) and click on **Install**.
   - Sign in to your Google Workspace account and allow Slack to access your Google tools (Gmail, Google Drive, Calendar, etc.).
2. **Sharing Google Files in Slack**
   - Once the integration is set up, you can share Google Drive files directly in Slack channels or direct messages.
   - Simply click the **Google Drive** button in the Slack message input box to search for and share files.
3. **Syncing Google Calendar with Slack**
   - Integrate your Google Calendar with Slack to receive event reminders, join video calls, and stay updated on upcoming meetings.
   - When you add the Google Calendar app to Slack, you can set up alerts and check your schedule from within Slack.

Integrating Google Workspace with Trello

1. **Add Google Drive Power-Up to Trello**
   - Open your Trello board and click on the **Power-Ups** button.

- Search for **Google Drive** and click **Add** to enable the integration.
2. **Attach Google Drive Files to Trello Cards**
   - Once the integration is activated, you can attach files from Google Drive directly to your Trello cards. This makes it easy to collaborate on tasks without leaving Trello.
   - Simply click **Attach File** on any card and select **Google Drive** to browse and add documents.

Integrating Google Workspace with Asana

1. **Add Google Drive Integration to Asana**
   - Open Asana and go to your workspace settings.
   - Select **Apps** and choose **Google Drive** to integrate it with Asana.
   - Grant Asana permission to access your Google Drive files.
2. **Attach Google Files in Asana Tasks**
   - When creating or editing tasks in Asana, you can attach Google Drive files, making it easy to keep all your resources organized within your task manager.

💡 *Tip: Integrating Google Workspace with tools like Slack, Trello, and Asana helps reduce switching between apps and creates a seamless workflow across platforms.*

Enhancing Productivity with Chrome Extensions

Google Chrome extensions are small tools that add functionality to your web browser, allowing you to improve productivity and enhance your Google Workspace experience. Many Chrome extensions integrate directly with Google Workspace apps, adding time-saving features and customization options.

Recommended Chrome Extensions for Google Workspace

1. **Google Keep Chrome Extension**
   - Install the **Google Keep** extension to quickly capture notes and ideas from any website.

- o   With this extension, you can save a webpage, add text, or create checklists directly to your Google Keep account.
2. **Google Drive Quick Create Extension**
   - o   The **Google Drive Quick Create** extension allows you to create new Google Docs, Sheets, and Slides from the Chrome toolbar with a single click.
   - o   This extension saves time and allows you to get straight to work without having to navigate through Google Drive.
3. **Grammarly for Google Docs**
   - o   **Grammarly** is a popular extension that helps you write more effectively by checking your grammar and spelling in real-time. It integrates with Google Docs and Gmail to provide suggestions as you write.
4. **Save to Google Drive Extension**
   - o   With the **Save to Google Drive** extension, you can save web content (such as images, videos, and text) directly to your Google Drive from Chrome, making it easy to organize and access important resources.
5. **Loom for Google Meet**
   - o   **Loom** allows you to record your screen and camera and share videos instantly. This extension is great for recording quick tutorials or meeting summaries during Google Meet calls.

💡 *Tip: Explore the Chrome Web Store for more extensions that can integrate with Google Workspace tools, such as project management apps, communication tools, or even productivity-enhancing features.*

PART 7: Troubleshooting & Expert Tips

Chapter 18: Common Google Workspace Problems & Fixes

While Google Workspace is a powerful suite of tools, users may occasionally encounter issues related to files, syncing, or connectivity. Knowing how to troubleshoot these common problems can save you time and frustration. In this chapter, we will address some of the most frequently reported issues in Google Workspace and provide practical solutions to resolve them.

Recovering Lost Files & Restoring Deleted Emails

Losing important files or emails can be a major inconvenience, but Google Workspace provides several ways to recover them.

Recovering Lost Files in Google Drive

1. **Check the Trash**
   - If you've accidentally deleted a file, it may still be in your **Google Drive Trash**.
   - To recover the file:
     - Open Google Drive and click on **Trash** in the left-hand menu.
     - Locate the file, right-click it, and select **Restore**.
2. **Use Google Drive Version History**
   - If you've lost data from an existing file, Google Drive allows you to revert to an earlier version.
   - To restore an older version of a file:
     - Right-click on the file and select **Manage versions**.
     - Choose the version you want to restore and click **Restore**.

3. **Google Drive Support**
    - o If the file is not in the Trash and version history doesn't help, try using the **Google Drive support** page for further assistance, especially if the file was deleted permanently.

Restoring Deleted Emails in Gmail

1. **Check the Trash**
    - o Gmail also has a **Trash** folder where deleted emails are stored temporarily.
    - o To recover deleted emails:
        - ▪ Open Gmail and click on **Trash** in the left sidebar.
        - ▪ Search for the email and select it. Then click on **Move to Inbox** to restore it.
2. **Using Gmail's Search**
    - o If you can't find the email in Trash, use Gmail's search bar with specific keywords or dates to locate the missing email.
3. **Gmail's "All Mail" Folder**
    - o If the email was archived instead of deleted, it will appear in the **All Mail** folder. Check here if you can't find the email in the Inbox or Trash.

💡 *Tip: Emails and files in Google Workspace are not lost permanently unless they are removed from Trash after 30 days. Always check your Trash folder first!*

Fixing Sync Issues with Google Drive & Calendar

Syncing problems can occur when your Google Drive or Calendar doesn't update across devices. Here are some ways to fix common syncing issues:

Google Drive Sync Issues

1. **Ensure You're Connected to the Internet**

- Google Drive syncs only when there's an active internet connection. Make sure your device is connected to the internet.
2. **Check Google Drive Storage**
   - If your Google Drive is full, new files won't sync. To check your storage:
     - Open Google Drive and check your storage usage at the bottom left corner.
     - If you're out of space, delete or move files to free up storage.
3. **Reinstall Google Drive (Backup & Sync)**
   - If sync issues persist, try reinstalling the **Google Drive Backup & Sync** application on your computer.
     - Uninstall the app, restart your computer, and then reinstall it from the Google Drive download page.
4. **Clear Cache & Cookies (Browser Users)**
   - If using Google Drive in your browser, clearing cache and cookies might resolve syncing issues. To do this:
     - Open your browser's settings, go to **Privacy & Security**, and click **Clear Browsing Data**. Ensure **Cookies and other site data** and **Cached images and files** are selected.

Google Calendar Sync Issues

1. **Check Calendar Settings**
   - Ensure your Google Calendar settings are configured correctly, and that sync is turned on. Go to **Settings** > **Accounts** > **Google** > **Sync Calendar**.
2. **Refresh the Calendar**
   - Sometimes, simply refreshing the calendar can fix sync issues. On your mobile device, swipe down on the calendar app to refresh, or click the **refresh** icon on the web version.
3. **Check Google Calendar Sync Settings**
   - Make sure that your Google Calendar is synced across devices by going into **Settings** and ensuring **Sync Google Calendar** is enabled.
4. **Update Your Google Calendar App**

- Make sure that you're using the latest version of the Google Calendar app. Go to the **App Store** (iOS) or **Google Play Store** (Android) and check for updates.

💡 *Tip: To troubleshoot syncing issues, always start by checking your internet connection and ensuring that your Google Workspace apps are up to date.*

Resolving Google Meet Connectivity Issues

Google Meet is an essential tool for video calls and meetings, but connectivity issues can disrupt communication. Here are some common solutions for resolving Google Meet connectivity problems:

Check Internet Connection

1. **Test Your Connection**
   - If your video or audio is lagging, check the stability of your internet connection. Use a speed test tool to ensure your connection meets Google Meet's requirements.
   - **Minimum Requirements for Google Meet:**
     - 3.2 Mbps for HD video
     - 0.5 Mbps for audio-only calls
2. **Switch to a Wired Connection**
   - If you're using Wi-Fi and experiencing issues, try switching to a wired connection for more stability.

Audio & Video Settings

1. **Check Audio and Video Settings**
   - Ensure that your microphone and camera are working properly. In **Google Meet**, click the three dots in the bottom-right corner, select **Settings**, and ensure that the correct microphone and camera are selected.
2. **Test Equipment**

o Test your microphone and camera with another app (e.g., Zoom, Skype) to rule out hardware issues.

Disable Background Apps & Tabs

1. **Close Other Tabs**
   o Close any unnecessary browser tabs or background apps that may be consuming bandwidth or causing your device to slow down.
2. **Disable Extensions**
   o Disable browser extensions that might interfere with Google Meet, especially ad blockers or security extensions.

💡 *Tip: If you're experiencing video issues, try turning off your camera temporarily or switching to an audio-only call to improve call quality.*

Chapter 19: Expert Tips & Hidden Features in Google Workspace

G oogle Workspace offers a wealth of features that can streamline your work, enhance productivity, and even surprise you with some hidden gems. In this chapter, we'll cover essential tips and tricks that can help you use Google Workspace more efficiently, plus some hidden features you might not know about.

Must-Know Keyboard Shortcuts for Faster Work

Keyboard shortcuts are a great way to speed up your workflow. They help you navigate Google Workspace apps quickly and without taking your hands off the keyboard.

Google Drive Shortcuts

- **New File**: Shift + T (Create a new document)
- **New Folder**: Shift + F
- **Search**: / (Quickly search within Google Drive)
- **Open File**: Enter (To open a selected file)
- **Move File**: Shift + Z (Move the file to a new location)

Gmail Shortcuts

- **Compose Email**: C (Start a new email)
- **Send Email**: Ctrl + Enter (Send an email)
- **Archive Email**: E (Archive the selected email)
- **Reply to Email**: R (Reply to the email)

- **Mark as Read**: Shift + I (Mark the selected email as read)
- **Label Email**: L (Label an email)

Google Calendar Shortcuts

- **Create Event**: C (Create a new event)
- **Next Day**: N (Move to the next day in the calendar view)
- **Previous Day**: P (Move to the previous day in the calendar view)
- **Day View**: 1 (Switch to Day view)
- **Week View**: 2 (Switch to Week view)

💡 *Tip: Learning these shortcuts can save you lots of time!*

Free Google Workspace Resources & Templates

Google Workspace comes with an extensive library of free templates and resources that you can take advantage of to improve productivity and creativity.

Google Docs Templates

- **Resume Templates**: Use pre-designed templates for professional resumes.
- **Project Proposals**: Templates for writing project proposals, business plans, and reports.
- **Business Letters**: Templates for formal business correspondence.

Google Sheets Templates

- **Budget Templates**: Start budgeting with a pre-set template for personal or business finances.
- **Invoice Templates**: Quickly create invoices for clients.
- **Gantt Charts**: Use Gantt chart templates to manage your project timelines.

Google Slides Templates

- **Presentation Themes**: Choose from a wide selection of themes to create professional presentations quickly.
- **Pitch Decks**: Find templates designed for creating investor presentations and pitch decks.

Google Forms Templates

- **Survey Forms**: Ready-to-use templates for creating surveys, quizzes, and questionnaires.
- **RSVP Forms**: Easy-to-use templates for event RSVP forms.

💡 *Tip: Google's template gallery is constantly updated, so always check back for new templates that can make your work easier.*

Latest Google Workspace Updates & Features

Google Workspace is continually evolving, and keeping up with the latest features ensures you're making the most of the tools at your disposal. Here are some of the newest updates and features in Google Workspace:

Google Meet Updates

- **Immersive View**: Google Meet has introduced an immersive view to make meetings more engaging by adjusting the background to fit multiple participants.
- **Live Translation**: Now, you can use Google Meet's real-time captions feature to translate conversations into different languages during video calls.

Google Drive Updates

- **Priority Page**: Google Drive has a new "Priority" page that automatically shows you the files you are most likely to need based on your past activity and interactions.

- **Smart Search**: Google Drive now has improved search functionality, allowing you to search for specific files more accurately with filters like "has a comment," "owner," or "created date."

Gmail Updates

- **Schedule Send**: Gmail now allows you to schedule emails to send at a specific time, ensuring that your emails land in the recipient's inbox at the most convenient moment.
- **Improved Search Filters**: Gmail has upgraded its search filters, so you can find emails even faster by searching by size, date, and attachments.

Google Docs Updates

- **Pageless Mode**: Google Docs now supports pageless mode, where the content flows without page breaks, making it ideal for long documents like reports or brainstorming notes.
- **Smart Compose**: Gmail's Smart Compose feature has been added to Google Docs, offering writing suggestions as you type, enhancing productivity and efficiency.

💡 *Tip: Keep an eye on the **Google Workspace Blog** for new updates and features. Google frequently rolls out enhancements to improve user experience.*

Index